Muriel Foster's Fishing Diary

A STUDIO BOOK
The Viking Press · New York

LITTLE LOCH BROOM AT SUNSET

MURIEL C. FOSTER

In Memory
of
JOHN KNOWLER

His last find
His first love

Published in 1980 by The Viking Press
625 Madison Avenue, New York, N.Y. 10022

Library of Congress Cataloging in Publication Data
Foster, Muriel, 1884-1963.
Muriel Foster's fishing diary.

(A Studio book)
1. Fishing—Scotland. I. Title. II. Title:
Fishing diary.
SH439.F77   1979   799.1'1'0941172   79-21156
ISBN 0-670-49557-3

Printed in Italy

The ngler, atte the least, hath his holsom walke and mery at his ease, a sweet ayre of the swete sauoure of the meede floures, that makyth him hungry; he heareth the melodyous armony of foules, he seeth the yonge swannes, heerons, duckes, cootes, and many other fowles, with their brodes; whyche me seemyth better than all the noyse of houndes, the blastes of hornys and the scrye of foulis, that hunters, fawkeners, and foulers can make.

nd if the angler take fysshe; surely, thenne, is there noo man merier than he is in his sporyte.

From "The Treatyse of Fysshynge wyth an Angle"

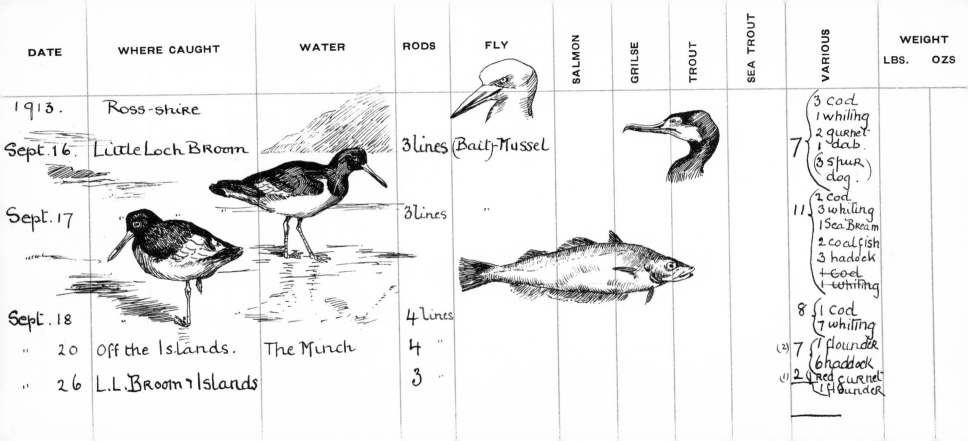

DATE	WHERE CAUGHT	WATER	RODS	FLY	SALMON	GRILSE	TROUT	SEA TROUT	VARIOUS	WEIGHT LBS.	OZS
1913.	Ross-shire										
Sept. 16.	Little Loch Broom		3 lines	(Bait) Mussel					7 { 3 cod 1 whiting 2 gurnet 1 dab. (3 spur) dog.		
Sept. 17			3 lines	"					11 { 2 cod 3 whiting 1 Sea Bream 2 coalfish 3 haddock + cod 1 whiting		
Sept. 18			4 lines						8 { 1 cod 7 whiting		
" 20	Off the Islands.	The Minch	4 "						(2) 7 { 1 flounder 6 haddock		
" 26	L. L. Broom & Islands		3 "						(1) 2 { Red gurnet 1 flounder		

2 Cod & 1 Whiting by Self.

(with Violet Firth & Colin)

1 cod & 1 whiting by self.

(with Violet Firth & Colin)

V.M.B.F. Colin Maclean,

Kenny McKenzie & self.

both by self (V.M.B.F. Colin
K. Mackenzie & self.)
V.M.B.F. Mrs Gainsford
& self.

DATE	WHERE CAUGHT	WATER	RODS	FLY	SALMON	GRILSE	TROUT	SEA TROUT	VARIOUS	WEIGHT LBS.	OZS.
1913											
Sept. 12	Dundonnell River	Upper Reaches	2	(WORM)			20			2	
" 22	Loch a charn		2	Minnow			2			1	4
" 24	" " "		2				2			1	8
" 25	" " "						-			-	
							24			4	12
1914 June 10	Hunstanton, Norfolk		2	Shrimping					2 dabs. 2 eels		
1915 May 24.	Heather Lochs. Faighn		2				1				
June 1	" " "		2				4				
June 5	" " "		2				2				

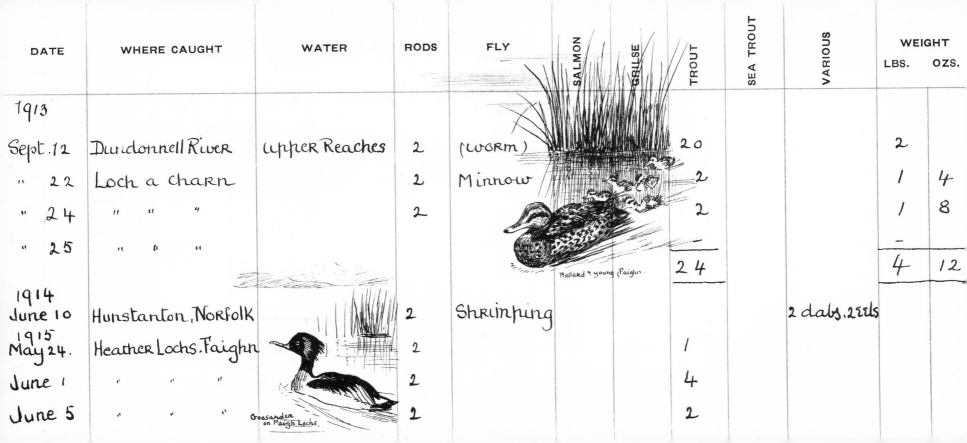

Mallard & young. Faighn.

Goosander on Faigh Lochs.

Violet Firth & self (my first trout - 7 -)

Dundas Firth & self (1 each)

Mrs Vickers (2) Self (0)

Rain & wind - Blank day -

Edward & self.

Hector Morrison (1) Self (0) & Y.M.B.F.

  "   "   (4) " (0) " "

  "   "   (2) " (0) " "

LITTLE LOCH BROOM AT SUNSET

DATE	WHERE CAUGHT	WATER	RODS	FLY	SALMON	GRILSE	TROUT	SEA TROUT	VARIOUS	WEIGHT LBS.	OZS.
1915.											
June 15	Dundonnell. Ross	Reedy Loch	2				4		4		
" 18	" "	"	2				1				
" 26	" "	Heather Lochs.	2				10				
" 29	" "	Reedy & another L. Loch na Fraoch,	2				1				
July 8	" "	Heather Lochs	2	March Brown			2				
" 13	" "	Loch a charn	2	Butcher			2			1	4
" 20	Dundonnell River		1	Black Doctor			1				
" 26	Faighn, Dundonnell	Loch an Blue	3	Butcher, Red Palmer			5				
Aug. 11	Loch a charn "	Loch a charn	2				1				

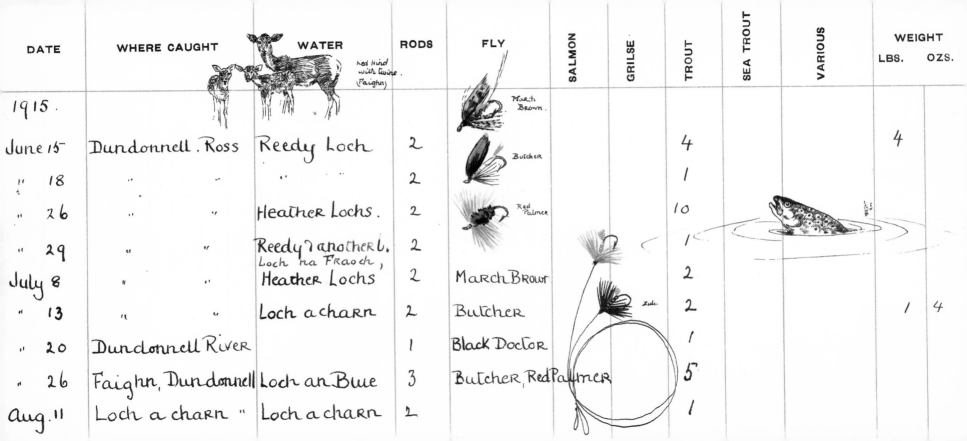

Red Hind with twins. (Faighn)

March Brown.

Butcher

Red Palmer

Zulu

The Mansion House. Dundonnell.

ector (4) self (0) ? V.M.B.F.

ector (1) self (0)

ector (9) self (1) my first on fly

ector (1) self (0)

M.B.F. self (1) Hector (1)

r Black Milne (2) self (0)

Beethoven "

Beethoven" (3) self (1) Mr Skinner 1 of 1½ lbs.

Mrs Bather (1) self (0)

DATE	WHERE CAUGHT	WATER	RODS	FLY	SALMON	GRILSE	TROUT	SEA TROUT	VARIOUS	WEIGHT LBS.	OZS.
1915											
Aug. 13.	Dundonnell River		1				2				
" 14		Upper reaches	1				5				
" 16			1				3				
" 17			1				1				
" 19			1	Black Doctor Claret & Grouse			7				12
" 19			1	(worm)			10				
" 24			1	Alexandra			9	—			
" 26	Dundonnell Ross.	Loch a charn	1	Zulu			1			1	12
" 27	"	River & L. na h'airbhe		Zulu (4) worm (3)			7				

Fly labels: Zulu, Alexandra, Claret & Grouse

Raven on Meall a charn.

Black Throated Diver
on Loch a Chann.

Hooked & Lost a sea Crout

First cast of the day

"Beethoven" (2) Tom Bather (1) Self (4)

DUNDONNELL. FROM A WATERCOLOUR BY F. MACKINNON.

DATE	WHERE CAUGHT	WATER	RODS	FLY	SALMON	GRILSE	TROUT	SEA TROUT	VARIOUS	WEIGHT	
										LBS.	OZS.
1915											
Aug. 30	Dundonnell River		1	Zulu & worm			6				
" 31	" "		2	Butcher Alexandra, worm.			13				
Sept. 1	" "		1	worm			2				
" 3	Dundonnell	Loch na h'airbhe	1				2				
" 4	" River	upper Reaches	1	Alexandra, worm.			5				
" 6	Dundonnell	Reedy Loch Burn	1	worm			8			1	4
" 9	Faighn, Dundonnell	Heather lochs	1	Zulu			3			1	2
" 14	Dundonnell River		1	Zulu & worm			6			1	10
" 16	" "		1				1				

Zulu

Alexandra.

Butcher.

Red Throated Diver on Faighn lochs.

A Dundonnell
Wild Cat.

Saw 'it' several times up
the Brae - they are not
uncommon here.

Beethoven (4) Self (9...

...old & wet

...urn very narrow in parts

...rilliant sunshine all day.

LITTLE LOCH BROOM FROM THE TOP OF THE BRAE.

DATE	WHERE CAUGHT	WATER	RODS	FLY	SALMON	GRILSE	TROUT	SEA TROUT	VARIOUS	WEIGHT LBS.	OZS.
1915											
Sept. 22	Dundonnell River		1				2				
June 30	Little Loch Broom		2						7 coalfish	57	
July 5	"								—		
July 23	"								—		
Sept. 2.	"		3						3 { 1 Gurnet 1 cod 1 flounder	2	4
Sept. 11	The Minch . Ross.	off the Islands	2						2 Haddock Whiting		
Sept. 25	Little Loch Broom								16 cod haddock		

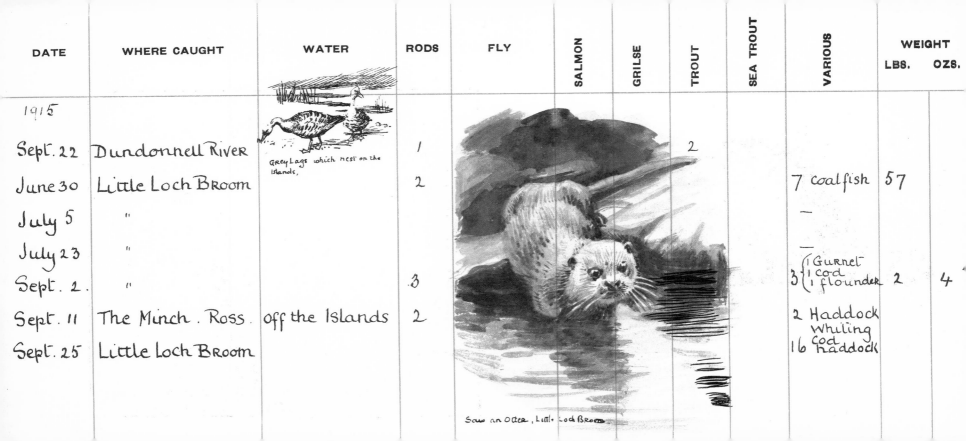

Grey Lags which nest on the Islands.

Saw an Otter, Little Loch Broom

Seal, off the Islands.

...olling, Hector (3) Self (4) about 10 lbs, 10 lbs, 10 lbs, 7 lbs, 5 lbs, 5 lbs.

...olling. The shoal had moved up the loch.

...oo Rough for hand lines

...om Bather, Colin & Self. (1 each)

Beethoven" (2) Self (0)

Dundonnell Total for 1915

	No	Caught by self.	Largest fish
Salmon	2	0	
Sea Trout	5	0	
Brown "	174	93	2 lbs. by Hector
Sea Fish	28	9	10 lb. coal fish by self.
	209	102	

Sea Fish. (12 Whiting, 4 haddock, 3 cod, 1 gurnet, 1 flounder, 7 coal fish.

DATE	WHERE CAUGHT	WATER	RODS	FLY	SALMON	GRILSE	TROUT	SEA TROUT	VARIOUS	WEIGHT LBS.	WEIGHT OZS.
1916											
May 12	Gruinard. R. Ross		6	Blue Zulu / Zulu.				1		1	4.
May 13	Dundonnell River		2				4				12
May 17	" "	upper Reaches	1				1				4
May 18	Gruinard River		4		1		1	1		1.0	4
May 26	Dundonnell River	upper Reaches	3	(worm) Zulu Small Jock Scott			30			3	8
June 30	" "		1				5				8
July 3	Dundonnell.	L. nam Badan Boga	3	Blue Zulu			7			9	
July 6	Faighr. Dundonnell	Heather Lochs.	3	Blue Zulu Teal & Red			10			4	
July 11	Dundonnell	L. nam Badan Boga	4				3			3	12

n Teallach

he Forge)

Emperor
Moth.

ector (1) V.M.B.F., Finlayson, Alan & Eleanor Mott & self (0)

E. Mott (3) self (1)

wet & rather cold

Finlayson 9½ lb salmon. Hector lost one after ¼ hr. E. Mott, sea trout ¾ lb. self (0)

Mr Carbonnell (8) E. Mott (6) Self (16)

nr Burcham - Rogers (3) Self (4) 1½ lbs, 1½ lbs, 1 lb. 3 oz, 1 lb. 1 oz.

nr Burcham - Rogers (2) Mrs Burcham - Rogers (2) Self (6)

nr Burcham - Rogers, Hector & Self 1 each (1¼ lbs each)

DATE	WHERE CAUGHT	WATER	RODS	FLY	SALMON	GRILSE	TROUT	SEA TROUT	VARIOUS	WEIGHT LBS.	OZS.
1916	(Gaelic, am Bad-call; The Hazel Clump.)			march Brown							
July 12	Badcaul. Ross	Loch an Gilich	3	Blue Zulu			11			2	
Aug. 4	Dundonnell R.		1				1				4
Aug 5	Dundonnell.	Loch na h'airbhe	2/	Zulu / Blue Zulu			5			1.	
Aug. 14	"	" " "	2/	Zulu / Blue Zulu			3				
Aug. 15	Dundonnell River	upper Reaches	1	(worm / small Jock Scott			3				8
Aug. 21	Dundonnell	Loch na h'airbhe	2	Blue Zulu			8			1	8
Aug 23		" "	2				3			1	12
Aug. 24	"na Fèithean-the Bog channels (Na Lochan Fraoich) " (faighn)	Heather Lochs	2	Claret & Grouse / Alexandra			4			1	8
Aug 28	Dundonnell River	Cottage Pool	1	Silver Doctor			28	1			6

My first Sea Trout.

MR & MRS Burcham - Rogers (4) Self (7)

ish Rising Short.

Dead calm

iver very low.

largest by Betty Bather with worm.

lf (0) & MR Bather (who put them into L. nam Badan Boga.

ll by MR Hewett, Self (0)

rew back 20 of them.   My first Sea trout!

Ola Bob.

DATE	WHERE CAUGHT	WATER	RODS	FLY	SALMON	GRILSE	TROUT	SEA TROUT	VARIOUS	WEIGHT LBS.	OZS.
1916											
Aug. 29.	Dundonnell River		1	Alexandra			6				
Sept. 1	" "		1	"			1				
" 2	" "	Below deer bridge / Canon 9 other Pools	1	(worm)			9				
" 4	" "	"	.1	"			10				
" 6	" "	"	1	"			5				
" 13	" "	Garden Pool.	1	"			3				14.
" 16	" "	Road Pool	1	very small Blue Doctor	1					5	10
" 20	" "	Cottage Pool.	1	Silver Doctor	1					5	10
Oct. 9	" "	3 lowest pools	1	medium Jock Scott				4		3	

My First Salmon!

The Brae
Dundonnell.

...ry cold, River too big & Rising.

...y first salmon, played it an hour. Gaffed by Colin.

...n trout Rod.

...Trout Rod. Largest 1½ lbs.

DATE	WHERE CAUGHT	WATER	RODS	FLY	SALMON	GRILSE	TROUT	SEA TROUT	VARIOUS	WEIGHT LBS.	OZS
1916											
Oct. 11	Dundonnell River	House & Cottage Pools	1	Alexandra				2		1	4
Oct. 16	" "	Bridge Pool .	1	—							
Oct. 17	" "	above Cottage Pool	1	Medium Jock Scott				1			8
May 30	Little Loch Broom		1	Rubber eel (black)					2 coal fish		11
June 13	" " "		2	" " (coloured)					14 " "	105	
June 23	" " "		1	" " "					2 " "	14	
July 20	" " "		1	mussel					1 Whiling		8
July 7	" " "		2	"					4 { Haddock Gurnet Cod whiting	3	8

Jock Scott

Hector.

Played fish of about 12 lbs, on Trout Rod, an hour, then lost it

Trolling. Gaffed by Hector

" V.M.B.F.(9) self.(5)

" , 9lbs, 5 lbs.

Only out a short time

Haddock (2lbs) cod, & gurnet by self. Whiting by V.M.B.F.

Little Loch Broom

DUNDONNELL TOTAL FOR 1916

	No	By self.	Weight.	By self.	Largest Fish
Salmon	7	2	50 lbs	$11\frac{1}{4}$ lbs	$10\frac{1}{2}$ lbs. by Hector
Sea Trout	24	9		$5\frac{3}{4}$	4 lbs. "
Brown "	167	100	$65\frac{1}{2}$	$22\frac{1}{2}$	$2\frac{1}{2}$ lbs " "
Sea Fish	41	13	245	64	12 lbs " "
	239	124		$103\frac{1}{2}$ lb	
Coal Fish	34	9	Largest	12 lbs	by Hector
Haddock	1	1	"	2 lbs	" M.C.F.
Gurnet	1	1	"	1 lb.	" "
Cod	2	1	"	$\frac{1}{2}$ lb	" "
Whiting	3	1	"	$\frac{1}{2}$ lb	" "

DATE	WHERE CAUGHT	WATER	RODS	FLY	SALMON	GRILSE	TROUT	SEA TROUT	VARIOUS	WEIGHT LBS.	OZS.
1917											
May 25	Dundonnell. Ross	L. nam Badan Boga	1	Alexandra			1				12
June 1	" "	L. on Top of Meall an Drean	1	Zulu			1			4	4
June 2	" "	Waterlily Loch	1	March Brown / Blue Zulu			4			5	12
" "	" "	L. na h'airbhe	1				6				
" 7	" "	Waterlily Loch	1	Olive Dun / Blue Zulu			2			2	8
" 15	" "	Challich Burn & River	1	Olive Dun / Blue Zulu			3				
" 16	" "	L. na h'airbhe	1	Zulu, Blue / Zulu & Alexandra			11			1	8
" 18	" "	" " "	1				1				
" 19		Reedy & L. an Eilean	2	Bloody Butcher			3			1	8

Close day. Fish not Rising well.

Cold, gusty day with showers.

1½ lbs, 1¼ lbs, 1¼ lbs, 1¼ lbs.

Hooked 2 more which took away flies (Zulu)

Small for Coal fish bait.

In the evening

Only fished there a short time

2 by Hector, Self (1)

DATE	WHERE CAUGHT	WATER	RODS	FLY	SALMON	GRILSE	TROUT	SEA TROUT	VARIOUS	WEIGHT	
										LBS.	OZS.
1917											
June 25	Dundonnell River		2				2			1	
" 27	Dundonnell	Reedy Loch	2	Blue Zulu (2)			3			2	
" 28	Dundonnell River		1	(worm)			14			1	12
July 2	" "		1	"			15			2	8
" 12	Dundonnell	(Loch of the soft, wet clumps.) L. nam Badan Boga	1	Blue Zulu			1			1	6
" 13	Dundonnell River	Upper Reaches	2	(worm)			15			1	10
" 16	" " & Burns	Chasm Pools.	2	"			13			1	12
" 25	Dundonnell	Reedy Loch Burn	2	"			12			1	12
Aug. 3	"	L. nam B.B. & small lochs	1	Zulu			3			4	

arger fish by Hector

ector (3) 9 Self (0)

with Murdo Mackenzie

by Self, 8 by Roddie McKenzie

6 " 7 " " " who hooked salmon or enormous trout, which nearly pulled him in, in Canon Pool

Roddie 9 Self.

Fine day, wind variable.

DATE	WHERE CAUGHT	WATER	RODS	FLY	SALMON	GRILSE	TROUT	SEA TROUT	VARIOUS	WEIGHT LBS.	OZS.
1917											
Aug 8	Dundonnell	L. na h'airbhe	1	Zulu Alexandra			6			1	
" 11	"	Ault na charn (Loch on Hill of Thorns)	2	(Worm			13			1	12
" 13	"	Loch on Meall an Drean	1	Zulu			1			4	4
" "	"	Reedy Loch	1	Zulu(6) Blue Zulu, Bloody Butcher			8			4	8
" 15	Dundonnell River	Embankment Pool (G. Coire-shaillidh = Corry of Falness)	1	Butcher				1		1	6
" 17	Dundonnell	Corrie Hallie Burn	2	(Worm)			19			2	8
" 18	"	Ault na charn	2	"			20			1	8
" 20	Dundonnell River	Sea Pools	1	medium Black Doctor, small Butcher				9		7	8
" "	" "	Bridge Pool	1				1				8

not Rising well.

Roddie (4) Self (9)

Heavy showers, thunder

'   ''   '

Thundery weather

Doris Seager (6) Self (13)

Doris Seager (6) Self (14) Small 7 very poor condition

2¼ lbs, 1½ lbs. Showers.

River moderately high.

Sea Pools, Dundonnell River

DATE	WHERE CAUGHT	WATER	RODS	FLY	SALMON	GRILSE	TROUT	SEA TROUT	VARIOUS	WEIGHT LBS.	OZS.
1917				Butcher							
Aug 21	Dundonnell River	Sea Pools	1	Teal & Red / Blue Doctor				5		3	
" 28	" "	Cattle Pool.	1	Butcher / Teal & Red (medium)				2		2	4
" 30	" "	below Shepherd's P.	1	Jock Scott				1		2	
" 31	" "	Bridge, House, Cottage	1	"				3		1	8
Sept. 3	Gruinard R. Ross.	Shepherd's Pool	2	Wasp?	1			1		18;1	8;4
" 5	Dundonnell	Reedy Loch	1				1	7		7	9
" 14	Dundonnell River	Embankment & House P.	1	small Jock Scott	-		2	1		1	1
" 18	" "	Sea Pool	1	Butcher				2		1	
" 20	" "	" "	1	Butcher etc.				4		4	4

Blue Doctor

Colin with Bob, Smoke, Ranger & Jandoc

...howers, River not very high.

...Vet, except for short interval

...Rain all day, River rising

...River big, but falling, fine, a little sunshine

...Hooked by Finlayson. I played it to the gaff. 18½ lbs

...Hazy sunshine, nice breeze, water very thick.

...Rose a salmon 3 times to same fly. High wind, showers, more rain coming

...Quantity of rising fish, either would not look at fly or rose short. Wind changed to W. for few minutes, caught 2 in 5 min

...Squally, wind S.W.

DATE	WHERE CAUGHT	WATER	RODS	FLY	SALMON	GRILSE	TROUT	SEA TROUT	VARIOUS	WEIGHT LBS.	WEIGHT OZS.
1917											
Sept 21	Dundonnell River	Sea Pool	1	Butcher				1			8
" 24	"	Embankment P.	1		1					4	14
" 26	"	Shepherd's Pool	1	Butcher				1			8
Oct. 4		" "	1	Jock Scott with blue hackle	1					18	
" "		Long Pool	1	"				2		2	6
" "		Hector's Pool	1	Teal & Red			1			1	10
" 6		Shepherd's "	1	Jock Scott	1					6	
" 9		Cattle "	1	" "	—				1	1	10

The White Stag of Dundonnell with the
Red stag which always accompanied it.
They were always low down the hills &
near the house. Aged years. Weight 16 stone 2 lbs.
7 points. (9 in 1915, 6 in 1916)

REMARKS

"BOB"

ind S.W. Sunshine, clouding over later, lost 3 other sea trout

aught between short, sharp showers.

Wind S.W. cloudy, getting gradually colder, ending in heavy rain. Fish rising short.

Played it for an hour. Gaffed, in the dusk, by Colin. River running high. Very cold, N.W. wind, and

showers of hail & rain. All fish same fly, except 1 sea trout

Wind N.W. Cold with hail showers. Bring alone, had to play it $\frac{3}{4}$ hr. before landing it with net. River fairly high.

Wind S. changing to N. Fine in morning, then heavy rain which lessened later. Lost a salmon

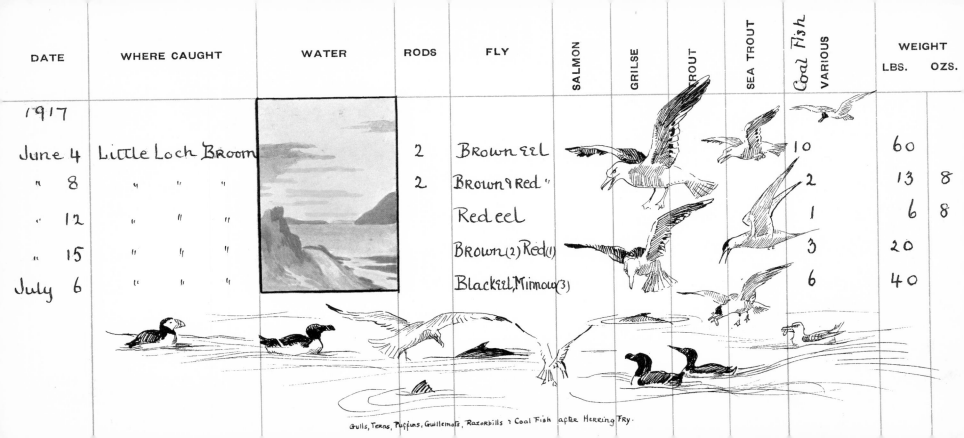

DATE	WHERE CAUGHT	WATER	RODS	FLY	SALMON	GRILSE	TROUT	SEA TROUT	Coal Fish / VARIOUS	WEIGHT LBS.	OZS.
1917											
June 4	Little Loch Broom		2	Brown eel					10	60	
„ 8	„ „ „		2	Brown & Red „					2	13	8
„ 12	„ „ „			Red eel					1	6	8
„ 15	„ „ „			Brown (2) Red (1)					3	20	
July 6	„ „ „			Black eel, Minnow (3)					6	40	

Gulls, Terns, Puffins, Guillemots, Razorbills & Coal Fish after Herring Fry.

REMARKS

Hector (1) Self (9) Thousands in the loch

" " " (1)

Other boats took a good many with black eel.

An immense number of fish in the loch this year, but

not taking well; tried Minnow, Trout, black, Red & brown eel.

Coal Fish or Suithe

DUNDONNELL TOTAL FOR 1917

Fish	No.	By self	Weight	by self	Largest fish.
Salmon	8	4	79½ lbs	34 lbs	18 lbs. by M.C.F
Sea Trout	38	35	33 lbs	30½	3 lbs " "
Brown "	184	147	52½ lbs	45	4¼ lbs " "
Coal Fish	22	19	140 lbs	120 lbs	7 lbs. " "
	252	205	305 lbs	229¼	

DATE	WHERE CAUGHT	WATER	RODS	FLY	SALMON	GRILSE	TROUT	SEA TROUT	VARIOUS	WEIGHT	
										LBS.	OZS.
1918	(Norse, grunna-fjördr = shallow firth)										
April 12	Gruinard River							3		3	4
May 22	Dundonnell	Waterlily Loch (L. of the Fence or Wall)	1	grey fly			1			1	8
" 28	"	L. na h'airbhe	1				6				12
June 28	Dundonnell River	Long Pool	1								12
" 29	Gruinard River	Otter Pool (Loch na t'raoich)	2	Blue bodied fly. Zulu	—						
July 9	Dundonnell	Heather Lochs (Yellow Loch)	1	Claret & Grouse			3			1	8
" 10	Faighn, Dundonnell	Loch an buie	1				1				4
" 16	Dundonnell River	House & Hector's Pool	1	Teal & Red cle			1	2		3	4
" 19	" "	Hector's Pool	1	small Silver Doctor			1			2	4

I think they may have been well mended kelts, silvery & in good condition. Wind changed to N. in afternoon.

Mist came down & made fishing impossible.

Fish rising short

Lost fish of about 7 lbs., after playing it some time.

Thunder, no fish showing.

Very warm, uncertain breeze, a good deal of thunder, fish rising, but would not take fly.

Warm & cloudy, threw back about 20 small trout

On trout rod, at dusk. Lost similar fish, on small Blue Doctor, in same place in the morning.

DATE	WHERE CAUGHT	WATER	RODS	FLY	SALMON	GRILSE	TROUT	SEA TROUT	VARIOUS	WEIGHT LBS.	OZS.
1918											
July 22	Dundonnell River	Bridge Pool	1	Silver Grey			1				4
" 24	" "	Cattle "	1	Blue bodied fly				1		2	
Aug. 6	Dundonnell	Heather Lochs	1	Zulu etc.			6			2	8
" 20	Dundonnell River	Cottage Pool	1	Small Butcher			1			2	8
" 26	"	Sea Pools	1	Small Silver Doctor				1			8
Sept. 4	"	House, Cottage & Embankment Pools	1	Small Jock Scott, Butcher			2	2		2	8
" 5	"	Sea Pool	1	Small Silver Doctor & Butcher				2			12
" 8	"	Bridge & Sea Pools	1	"	1		7	1		4	8

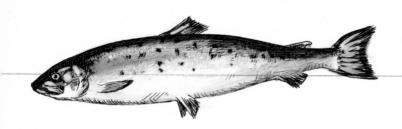

REMARKS

Ran from top of pool to shingle below it.

Warm & cloudy.

Warm & cloudy, fish moving, but not taking fly well. Lost 1 on Butcher

Cloudy, cleared later. River moderately high.

N.W. Bright sunshine, River low.

DUNDONNELL TOTAL. 1918.

Fish.	No.	By self.	Weight.	By self.	Largest fish.
Salmon	2	—	19 lbs	—	13 lbs. by Hector
Grilse	1	1	4 "	4 lbs	4 lbs. by M.C.F
Sea Trout	16	14	19 "	16½ "	2½ lbs " "
Brown "	38	22	11¼ "	8½ "	1½ lbs " "
	57	37	53¼ lbs	29 lbs	

DATE	WHERE CAUGHT	WATER	RODS	FLY	SALMON	GRILSE	TROUT	SEA TROUT	VARIOUS	WEIGHT LBS.	OZS.
1919											
May 28	Dundonnell	Loch na h'airbhe	1	Teal & Red			4				
June 14	Dundonnell River	Cottage Pool	1	Butcher			2	1			8
" 16	" "	Cottage & Hector's	1	Butcher etc			3				8
" 17	Dundonnell	Reedy Loch	1	Zulu			3			1	
" 24	Dundonnell River	Bridge & House P.	1	Teal & Red Silver Doctor			3				8
" 26	Dundonnell	L. na h'airbhe	1	Zulu			1				4
" 30	" River	Shepherd and Bridge Pools.	2	Zulu, Blue Zulu			2			1	
July 10	Taighn, Dundonnell	Heather Lochs	1	Teal & Red			9			3	12
" 21	" "	Loch an buie	1	Teal & Red			2			1	12

Redshank

Lost a good fish in Loch nam Badan Boga. Fish not showing

Only fishing for about an hour.

Sea trout very small. Misty rain all day

River in splendid order, but fish not up yet.

Turned wet & thundery. Fish not taking in L. nam Badan Boga.

Hector ($\frac{3}{4}$ lb) Self ($\frac{1}{4}$) fish not up yet.

Warm, with a nice ripple.

Calm & warm at first, then colder & very heavy showers.

DATE	WHERE CAUGHT	WATER	RODS	FLY	SALMON	GRILSE	TROUT	SEA TROUT	Coal fish	VARIOUS	LBS.	OZS.
1919												
July 31	Dundonnell River	upper Reaches Cottage, Bridge	2	(worm) small Silver			11				1	10
Aug. 1	" "	& Cattle Pools	2	Doctor, Jock Scott				3			3	11
" 6	Dundonnell	L. na h'airbhe	2	Teal & Red Zulu			3					8
" 9	" River	Cattle Pool.	1	small Silver Doctor.				1			1	12
June 20	Little Loch Broom	off Ardessy	1	Brown Eel.						2	15	
July 1	" " "	Boat House to Kildonan	1	Red & black Eels						7	5 6	
July 7	" " "		1	Black Eel						2	14	
July 9	" " "		1	" "						1	8	
Aug. 11	Dundonnell	Loch a charn	1	Butcher			1					5

"Luna"

Eileen Bruce (3) Self (8)

Hector (1 ¾ lbs) 9 Self (1 lb. 100 g.; 5 oz.)

Self (2) Eileen (1) misty Rain. no Rise.

Warm. River low.

Only came upon tail end of shoal.

Fish not showing at all, but taking well.

High wind. Warm. Fish not moving.

DATE	WHERE CAUGHT	WATER	RODS	FLY	SALMON	GRILSE	TROUT	SEA TROUT	VARIOUS	WEIGHT	
										LBS.	OZS.
1919				Blue Minnow							
Aug. 12	Dundonnell	Loch a charr	1	Olive Dun			4			1	10
" 13	"	River Bridge Pool	1	Silver Doctor			1				3
" 16	"	Reedy Loch	1	Zulu, Olive Dun, Blue Doctor			2			2	12
" 18	"	River Shepherds & Long Pool.	1	Silver Doctor, Black " Black Doctor			3				9
" 21	"	" Bridge, cattle, Hectors & Long Pools	3	"Reid" for S.T.			1	3		37	14
" 22	"	" Hector's Pool	1	Teal & Red			1	1		2	8
" 25	"	Reedy Loch	1	Olive Dun			1				7
" 28	"	River Bridge, Road & House Pools	1	Jock Scott, S... Black Doctor			1	2		7	6
Sept. 1	"	" House Pool	1				1				6

REMARKS

Golden Eagles.

High wind fish not showing much.

River low. Saw 2 Sea trout which would not take fly.

Warm & cloudy. Later, thunder clouds put fish down. ($1\frac{3}{4}$ lbs.; 1 lb)

Frequent very heavy showers.

$1\frac{1}{2}$ lbs.; 1 lb 2 oz. by self, $\frac{1}{2}$ lb. by Henry Mott. I lost 2 good sea trout & a grilse. Grilse $4\frac{1}{2}$ lbs. by Hector

Pool rather low & very clear, used fine cast & small fly.

E. wind. Fish not rising well. Gale & heavy rain the following night.

River in good order but very clear. Grilse 3 lbs 6 oz. Largest Sea Trout 2 lbs. 7 oz.

"Dirty days hath September,
April, June and November.
From January up to May,
The rain it raineth every day.
All the rest have thirty-one,
Without a blessed gleam of sun,
And, if any of them had two-and-thirty,
They'd be just as wet and twice as dirty!"

DATE	WHERE CAUGHT	WATER	RODS	FLY	SALMON	GRILSE	TROUT	SEA TROUT	VARIOUS	WEIGHT LBS.	OZS.
1919											
Sept. 2	Dundonnell River	Deer Bridge to Chasm.	3	(worm)			10			1	12
" 6	"	Reedy Loch	1	Olive Dun			2				8
" 8	"	Loch na h'airbhe	2	Zulu / Olive Dun			6			1	3
" 9	" (Taighn)	Heather Lochs	2	Zulu (6) / (Teal? Red(5))			14			7	4
" 10	" "	"	2	Zulu / Olive Dun.			2			1	4
" "	" River	above Taighn Bridge	1	Bloody Palmer			5			1	2
" 17	"	L. na h'airbhe	1				1				3
" 22	" River	Long Pool	1	Jock Scott	—						
" 23	" "	Cottage and Cattle Pools	1	" "				3		3	5

"LUNA"

Bridge Pool. Dundonnell River

"LUNA"

Not fishing very long. V.M.B.F. (2) Eileen (3) Self (5) Fine & warm.

Fish showing, but not taking the fly well.

Mr. Carbonnell (1) Self (5) Wind very variable. Rain.

Mr. Carbonnell (2) Self (12) including 8 of about $\frac{3}{4}$ lb. each.

Wind S. very strong. Mr Carbonnell $\frac{3}{4}$ lb. self $\frac{1}{2}$ lb. Fish not rising well.

Fished for an hour, fish rising well, threw back 6.

Fish not rising at all on L. nam Badan Boga.

Hooked & lost 2 in Long Pool, rose one in Bridge Pool. Cold & showery, River big.

River smaller. Cold & showery.

DATE	WHERE CAUGHT	WATER	RODS	FLY	SALMON	GRILSE	TROUT	SEA TROUT	VARIOUS	WEIGHT	
										LBS.	OZS.
1919		Shepherd's and Cattle		Silver Grey,							
Sept. 26	Dundonnell River	Long Pools	1	Jock Scott				5		3	
" 27	" "	Road Pool	1	"				1		1	10
" 29	" "	Cattle and Cottage Pools	1	" and Butcher				2			14
" 30	" "	Cattle, House T above Cottage Pools	1	Teal & Red Black Doctor				3		2	4
Oct. 2.	" "	Bridge Pool to Deer Bridge.	2	(Worm)			13	#3		2	8
" 3	"	Reedy Loch Burn	2	"			15	F		2	2
" 6	" River	Hector's, Shepherd's, Cattle & Bridge Pools.	1	Silver Doctor Jock Scott Black, silver body spider	1			4		9	8
" 14	" "	Shepherd's T Cottage Pools.	1	Jock Scott	1					7	8
	" "		"	"	1			1			8

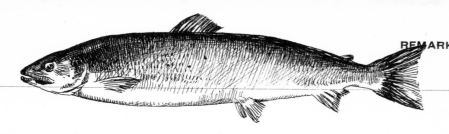

REMARKS

u Fresh Run. Bright morning. Heavy rain later

Wind N.W. Heavy hail showers.

Wind S. very high. Rain in morning, clear later.

Wind S. warm, misty Rain. River low. Trout rod, small flies

Mr. & Mrs Carbonnell (4) Self (9) Wind S. to S.W.

Mr Carbonnell (2) Self (13) Threw back a lot.

Wind S. warm & sunny.   Gaffed in 12 minutes Fresh Run

Fresh Run Hooked & lost 3 others on Jock Scott etc. Salmon 7 lbs.

Heavy hail showers. Landed salmon (without a gaff) by myself, in 10 minutes. Sea Trout Fresh Run, but not salmon.

DUNDONNELL. 1919

Fish	No	By self.	Total Weight	caught by self.	Largest Fish.	
Salmon	3	2	23½ lbs	14½ lbs	9 lbs.	by Hector
Grilse	2	1	7¾ lb	3¼ lb	4½ "	" "
Sea Trout	31	27	31 lb. 3 oz	25 lb 15 oz	2½ lbs	" M.C.F.
Brown "	279	107	57 lbs	32 lb 5 oz	2½ lbs	" Mr Carbonnell.
Coal Fish	12	12	93	93	8 lb	" M.C.F.
	327	149	212 lb. 7 oz	169 lbs		

DATE	WHERE CAUGHT	WATER	RODS	FLY	SALMON	GRILSE	TROUT	SEA TROUT	VARIOUS	WEIGHT LBS.	WEIGHT OZS.
1920											
May 31	Leckmelm. Ross.	Lochanan Thiodha	1	Butcher							7
June 2	Broom River	March Pool	1	Jock Scott	1					11	8
" 26	Leckmelm. Ross.	Lochanan Thiodha / Loch Maire Dhonn	1	Butcher			1				
" 28	" "	Lochanan Fiodha	1	Zulu (8)			6		2		
July 5	" "	" "	1	Claret & Grouse			3				Small "
" 12	Loch Broom Glebe	Loch an Tiompain	1	Butcher			4				
" 14	Leckmelm. Ross.	Lochanan Fiodha	2	Zulu, Butcher a light fly			8			1	14
" 17	Broom River. Ross	Middle Pool	1	Red Spider					1		
" 24	" " "	March Pool	2	Jock Scott					1		

Butcher

Zulu

Claret Grouse

Cold, driving mist, high wind. (Loch Leven Trout)

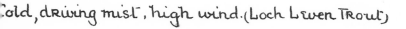

Fisherman's
Knot
(single)

argest 14 oz.

Black Rabbit (Leckmelm.)

R. Black-Milne (3) largest $\frac{3}{4}$ lb, self (5)

ooked & lost 2 large sea Trout or Grilse on Red Palmer.

Fannich Hills from Leckmelm.

DATE	WHERE CAUGHT	WATER	RODS	FLY	SALMON	GRILSE	TROUT	SEA TROUT	VARIOUS	WEIGHT LBS.
1920				Jock Scott						
Aug 4	Broom R. Ross-shire	Middle Pool	2	Trout fly				1		8.
" 7	Loch Broom Glebe.	L. an Tiompain (Loch of the Fir Trees)	2	Zulu, Wood- -cock & Yellow			2			
" 14	Leckmelm. Ross.	Lochan an Tiodha	2	Trolling, Black eel (3) Spoon, minnow			3			
July 1	Loch Broom		2 lines	(Hand lines) Red eel (1) spoon (2)					7 coal fish	49
" 6	" "	(Field of the crossing)	3 lines	bait mussell					20 { 3 Whiting (14) Cuddie, Flounder + Spur dog	32
" 13	" "	Raon a chroisg	1	Silver minnow					1 Lythe	small
" 15	" "		3 line	mussel.					24	6 (about)
" 20.	" "	off Black Rock	3 lines	"					25	10 (about)
" 27	"	" " "	3 lines	"					3	1

REMARKS

Beresford Bruce (1) I rose a salmon 3 times.

Beresford & Self.

Major Mothersill and Self.

Eileen Bruce(4) Self(3) Fish showing but very stiff to take. Lost 2 on minnow, 1 on Black Eel.

Eileen, Colin & Self.

Trolling with Rod.

Mostly Haddock & whiting

"   "   "   & a good size.

Next boat (to which we tied) caught 60 (4 lines)

Grey Gurnet.   Codling
Whiting .   Haddock
Coal Fish .   Miller

DATE	WHERE CAUGHT	WATER	RODS	FLY	SALMON	GRILSE	TROUT	SEA TROUT	VARIOUS	WEIGHT	
										LBS.	OZS.
1920									1 Flounder / 1 Cod / 3 Haddock / 26 Whiting / 2 Miller		
Aug. 5	Loch Broom. Ross		3 lines	mussel.					32	6	
„ 10	„ „ „			„					73 { 67 Whiting / 2 Flounder / 1 Haddock / 1 codling etc / 1 miller 1 cuddie	12	
„ 12	„ „ „		3 lines	„					37 { 2 Haddock / 2 Flounder / 2 gurnet / 31 Whiting	6	
„ 16	The Minch. Ross.	Off Carn nan Sgeir (Cairn - Skerry)	5 lines	„					18 { Haddock / cod (1)	14	
„ 17	Loch Broom „	„ The Gale	4 lines.	„					14 { Haddock / Whiting / Codling (1) / Gurnet (3)	4	8
„ 20	„ „ „	Bay near pier	2 lines	„					7 { 2 Flounders / 4 codling / 1 cuddie	2	8
„ 21	The Minch „	Between Tanera & Black Island.	2 lines	„					4 { 2 Haddock / 1 Grey Gurnet / 1 miller	1	8
„ 23	Loch Broom „	Black Rock & gale	4 lines	„					24 { 21 whiting / 1 haddock / 2 miller	5	
„ 30	„ „ „	The Gale	3 lines	„					61 { 57 whiting / 1 codling / 1 gurnet / 2 millers	10	

Goosander.

Loch Broom from Leckmelm.

Beresford Bruce (14) Colin (13) Self (5) I lost a big cod.

Self (25) The next boat caught 120.

Beresford (16) Colin (3) Self 18. 1 whiting took both hooks.

Eileen, (5, the largest a $1\frac{3}{4}$ lb Haddock) Fernie, (2) & Beresford Bruce (2) Kenny-Ferry ((6) largest cod of 3 lbs) self (3)

Beresford (5) Fernie (1) Colin (2) self (6) largest $1\frac{3}{4}$ lb coaling.

      "   (5) Self (2)

Kenny-Ferry - (2) self (2)

Beresford (5) Colin and Duncan Maclean (6) Self (13)

Duncan, Colin & Self (16)

Loch Broom by moonlight.

DATE	WHERE CAUGHT	WATER	RODS	FLY	SALMON	GRILSE	TROUT	SEA TROUT	VARIOUS	WEIGHT LBS.	OZS.
1920		Burn & Bay									
Sept. 1	Loch Broom. Ross	Black Rock & Gate	3 lines	"Miller" cut up.					60 { 2 codling / 56 Whiting / 1 miller / 1 cuddie	10	
" 2	" " "	The Gate, B. Rock	4 lines	mussel					28 { 20 whiting / 4 cuddie / 4 codling	5	12
" 4	" " "	Gate to near Slip Burn & Bay. off Rhiroy	2 lines	"					11 { 3 cuddie / 1 miller / 7 codling	2	4
" 7	" " "	Black Rock & Gate	4 lines	"					11 { 1 Haddock / 1 Flounder / 5 whiting / 3 codling / 1 Rockcod	4	
" 8	" " "	Black Rock & Bay	3 lines	"					6 { 5 codling / 1 Rock cod	1	8
" 9	" " "	Bay and Burn (Ruigh. Ruadh = Red hill Reach)	4 lines	"					7 { 2 whiting / 5 codling	1	8
" 13	" " "	Rhiroy - Gate	4 lines	"					40 { 28 Whiting / 7 Codling / 5 cuddie	12	
" 14	" " "	Well- Gate, & Bay	2 lines	"					6 { codling / cuddie	1	12
" 15	" " "	Well- Gate & Bay	3 lines	"					11 { 1 Gurnet / 1 cuddie / 2 whiting / 7 codlins	4	
" 17	" " "	Logie Bay. Burn	4 "	"					22 { 17 whitins / 1 coalfish, & miller	6	8

Loch an Tiompain, "The Loch of the White Fairy"

Beresford (19) Simon McLean (21) Self (20) used Miller cut up as bait, most successful.

Beresford (8) Self (11) Fernie & Simon.

Simon (4) Self (7) very shallow water, lost a big cod.

Self (8) Beresford, Eileen & Simon. Rock codling very red in colour.

" (3) " " " . Threw back small cuddies

Fernie , " , " & Self (0) very wet evening. Threw back small cuddies

Self (10) " . " and Simon. Sailed in the dinghy to Rhikoy & back

Very stormy. Beresford (3) Self (3)

Self (6) Beresford & Eileen. Gurnet ¾ lb. whiting over ½ lb.
♥ " " " & V.M.B.F. Beresford caught 1½ lb coalfish .

Fish.	No.		Weight.	
	Total.	By self.	Total	Largest
Salmon	1	1	11½ lbs	11½ lbs
Sea Trout	3	2	1½ lbs	½ lb
Brown "	51	23	11 lbs?	14 oz.
Coal Fish	10	4	70 lbs	70 lbs
Codling	68			3 lbs
Rock Cod	2			
Cuddie	20			1½ lbs
Haddock	42	189	138¼	1¾ "
Whiting	382			½ "
Grey Gurnet	8			¾ "
Lythe	1			
Flounder	11			
Miller	14			
	613	219	232¼ lbs	

TOTAL 1920

DATE	WHERE CAUGHT	WATER	RODS	FLY	SALMON	GRILSE	TROUT	SEA TROUT	VARIOUS	WEIGHT	
										LBS.	OZS.
1921.											
March 14	Broom River. Ross.	March Pool (Brown Mary's Loch)	1	Jock Scott	—						
May 21	Leckmelm. "	L. maire Dhonn	3				1				
" 23	Loch Broom Glebe	Loch an Fhion Loch an Tiompain (Loch of the Cairn.	3				3			3	
" 28	" " "	Loch a charn (Loch of the Plain)	3	small spoon			1				11
June 4	Moy. Inverness-shire	Moy Loch.	3	Watson's Fancy the			7			1	12
" 5	Findhorn River		3	Watson's Fancy Blue Zulu			1				
July 4	Loch Broom Glebe	(L. of the White Fairy) L. an Tiompain	1	Watson's Fancy?			3				
" 9	" " "	" "	3	Watson's Fancy			18				
" 16	" " "	" "	3	Blue Zulu Watson's Fancy			13				

Leckmelm Lodge.

Summer Isles. Loch Broom.

Trying to gaff it myself, lost it after getting it to edge of bank.

Tom Ferguson. V.M.B.F. & Self.

Tom Ferguson (1 of over 1½ lbs) Violet & Self (2) of under 1½ lbs)

Tom, Violet & Self. Wind N.

" " " (5) averaging about ¼ lb.

" " " River too low. Saw salmon rising.

Only fished 1½ hours.

Tom, Violet & Self. Big rise from 9.30 - 11 p.m.

Mr & Mrs Burcham-Rogers & Self (6) His largest 1 lb. from a small loch.

DATE	WHERE CAUGHT	WATER	RODS	FLY	SALMON	GRILSE	TROUT	SEA TROUT	VARIOUS	WEIGHT LBS.	OZS.
1921											
July 21	Leckmelm. Ross.	The Lochs	1	Watson's Fancy			2				
" 27	Broom River. "	Middle Pool.	3	Kingfisher				2			
June 18	Loch Broom	around Ullapool	3						6 {Haddock Codling Flounder Whiting}		
July 2	" "	" "							7 {Haddock codling}		
" 14	" "	Ullapool to Isle Martin							23 {5 mackerel Haddock Cod Rocke. coal fish Lythe}		
" 28	" "	" " " "							16 {1 Lythe 3 codling 9 mackerel cuddie Haddie}		
" 28	" "	" "							4		

(Gaelic, Loch Bhraoin

= Lake of Showers)

These Red codling, called locally, Rock codling,
are not uncommon in Loch Broom, they vary
much in the intensity of the colour which is
probably due to the feeding.

Mackerel -

Mackerel.

Fish rising short.

Mr & Mrs Burcham-Rogers (2) Self (0) lost several. Fished 1½ hrs.

Mr. & Mrs Burcham-Rogers & self. I lost a big lythe which snapped trace.

"   "   "   "   ". Wind N.W. Bright sunshine.

Coal fish of about 8 lbs & some big haddies. Mr & Mrs. B-R. & self.
                by self.

Cod of about 7 lbs by self. Mr & Mrs Burcham-Rogers & self.

Fish	No	Largest Fish
TOTAL FOR **1921**		
Brown Trout	49	1½ lbs.
Sea Trout	2	
Codling		7 lbs
Rock "		
Coal Fish		8 lbs
Haddock	52	
Lythe		
Whiting		
Mackerel		
	103	

DATE	WHERE CAUGHT	WATER	RODS	FLY	SALMON	GRILSE	TROUT	SEA TROUT	VARIOUS	WEIGHT LBS.	OZS.
1922											
(Jan 19)	(R. Granta . Cambs)	(above Mill.)		Watson's Fancy							
May 13	Findhorn R. Inverness		2	March Brown			3			1	9
" 31	Loch a charn	Loch a charn	3				4			2	4
June 6	Loch Broom Glebe	Loch an Tiompain	1	Artificial grub.			1			small	
" 7	" " "	Loch a charn	1	Nymph			1			"	
" 9	" " "	L. an Tiompain	1	Dry Fly.			4			+	r
" 14	" " "	Loch an Thiona	1	March Brown olive Dun			2			1	8
" 15	" " "	Loch a Mhill	1				−				
" 16	" " "	Loch a charn	2				1				5

Found a trout of over 16", caught under ice & stranded on the mud when the flood gates were opened.

Tom Ferguson & self. Fish rising greedily to a hatch of March Browns, would not take artificial fly.

Mr Sutherland, self & Reid (4 on a worm. All so gorged with shrimps   )

"Ben"

Dead calm, much of the time

misty rain most of the day.

Too bright and calm. Rose an enormous trout, could see it clearly. Rise of very big trout.

Thick, driving mist. Annie Sutherland (1) Self (0) Mr Bayne rowing.

DATE	WHERE CAUGHT	WATER	RODS	FLY	SALMON	GRILSE	TROUT	SEA TROUT	VARIOUS	WEIGHT LBS.	OZS.
1922											
June 24	Loch Broom Glebe	L. an Tiompair	1	Zulu artificial grub(?)			2				
" 26	" " "	" " F'hiona	1	Bloody Butcher			4				
Aug. 12	Dover Harbour	by the "Glatton"	4 lines	mussels					18 {Pouting Plaice}	small	"
" 14	" "	" " "	" "	"					23 Pouting	"	
" 15	" "	Off the Boom.	2 "	"					9 "	"	
" 16	" "	Off the "Glatton"	3 .	"					7 {Pouting Flounder}	"	
" 17	" "	Off Prince of Wales Pier (Admiralty)		"					13 {2 Golden Head, 8 Pouting, 2 Weaver, 1 Wrasse}	"	
" 19	" "	Off far Buoys.		"					4 {Flounder, Pouting(2)}	"	
" 21	" "	2nd Buoy from Boom		"					9 {Flounder, Pouting}		

Weather fearful. Heavy Rain. short intervals.

Mist & Rain . Cold .

Edward (9) Rodney (2) self (6) Paul (the Boatman)

" (14) " (3) " (4) Ronald (2)

" (2) " (2) " (5)

" (6) Ronald (1)

" (7) " (2) " (4)

George (1) " (3)

" (2) " (7)

The Hut.

DATE	WHERE CAUGHT	WATER	RODS	FLY	VARIOUS	WEIGHT	
						LBS.	OZS.
1922							
Aug 22	Dover Harbour 2nd Buoy & Boom			mussel.	4 { Plaice Pouting.	1	6

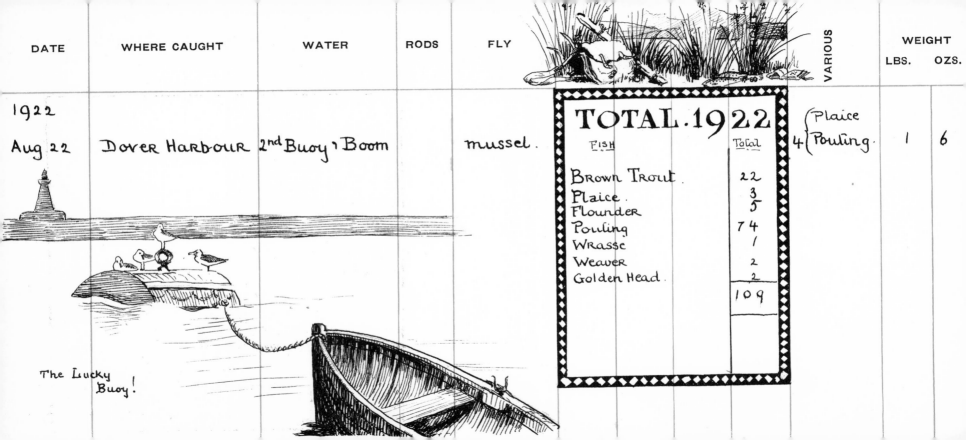

The Lucky Buoy!

TOTAL · 1922

FISH	Total
Brown Trout.	22
Plaice.	3
Flounder	5
Pouting	74
Wrasse	1
Weaver	2
Golden Head.	2
	109

WRasse

LesseR Weaver

Pouting.

Plaice

In DoveR HaRbouR.

DATE	WHERE CAUGHT	WATER	RODS	FLY	SALMON	GRILSE	TROUT	SEA TROUT	VARIOUS	WEIGHT LBS.	OZS.
1923	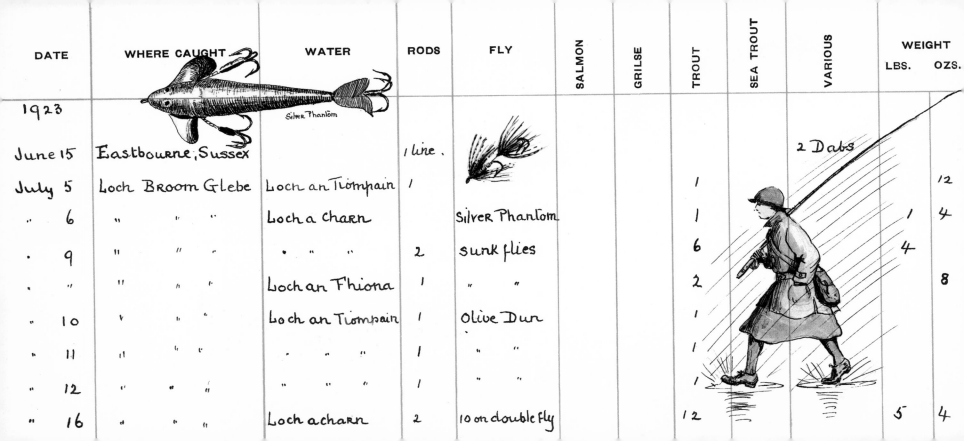										
June 15	Eastbourne, Sussex		1 line .						2 Dabs		
July 5	Loch Broom Glebe	Loch an Tiompain	1				1				12
„ 6	„ „ „	Loch a charn		Silver Phantom			1			1	4
. 9	„ „ „	. „ „	2	sunk flies			6			4	
„ „	„ „ „	Loch an Fhiona	1	„ „			2				8
„ 10	„ „ „	Loch an Tiompain	1	Olive Dun			1				
„ 11	„ „ „	„ „	1	„ „			1				
„ 12	„ „ „	„ „	1	„ „			1				
„ 16	„ „ „	Loch a charn	2	10 on double fly			12			5	4

REMARKS

Loch an Fhiona at midnight.

Turned very cold, wet & windy. Only out a short time.

Very late season. Hill lochs hardly started.

Very close & thundery. Hooked & lost a good one. Under Meall a charn

Annie Sutherland (3) self (3) largest 1¼ lbs, lost others rising short. Not showing at all, bottom feeding on shrimps, larvae and

10 - 11·30 P.M. Rising short. (crustaceans. Fish in this loch very red in the flesh, often redder than salmon.

11·45 P.M. Fish rising short. Off reeds.

about 10·30 P.M. " " "

No fish showing. Flies deeply sunk. Annie Sutherland (4) self (8) Colin Rowing.

LUNCH TIME!

DATE	WHERE CAUGHT	WATER	RODS	FLY	SALMON	GRILSE	TROUT	SEA TROUT	VARIOUS	WEIGHT LBS.	OZS.
1923											
July 18	Broom R: Ross-shire	Tail of the Bank	1							1	12
" 20	" " "	" " " "	1							1	2
" 21	" " "	Sea Pool .	1								8
" 23 .	Loch Broom Glebe	Loch an Tiompain	1	Blue Zulu							
" 27	Broom River .	Tail of the Bank	1	Jock Scott							8
" 28	" "	Sea Pool	1							1	13
" 30	" "	" Tail of Bank	2							1	15
" 31	" "	Sea Pool .	1	Silver Doctor Black Fly.						3	8
" "	Loch Broom .	SWEEP NET							49 (45 Mackerel, 1 Sea Trout, 1 Flounder, 3 cuttle fish).	3 5	4

REMARKS

Rising short.

S.E. Rising short. Rose a good many. Hooked 4.

Wet most of day. Finnock Rose at about 10.30 P.M.

Cold, wet, misty & altogether beastly. No fish Rising.

A great deal of Rain. Fish Rising short.

Close & thundery. 14 sea trout Rose - short - to me. Mr. S. 1 sea trout.

A good deal of Rain, Mr Sutherland (3) Self (4)

Largest 1½ lbs.

Also caught lots of jelly fish. Came in at midnight & cooked mackerel for supper.

THE HUT.

DATE	WHERE CAUGHT	WATER	RODS	FLY	SALMON	GRILSE	TROUT	SEA TROUT	VARIOUS	WEIGHT LBS.	WEIGHT OZS.
1923.											
Aug 4	Nairnside, Daviot	Pond	2	Watson's Fancy Gnat			5			1	12
" 6.	" " (Inverness)	"	1	"			2				8
" 8	" "	"	1	"			1				7
" 10	" "	"	2 1	Watson's Fancy March Brown			2			1	
" 11	" "	"	1	Dry Fly			1				
" 13	" "	"	2 1	" "			2				
" 14	" "	"	1	" "			1				8

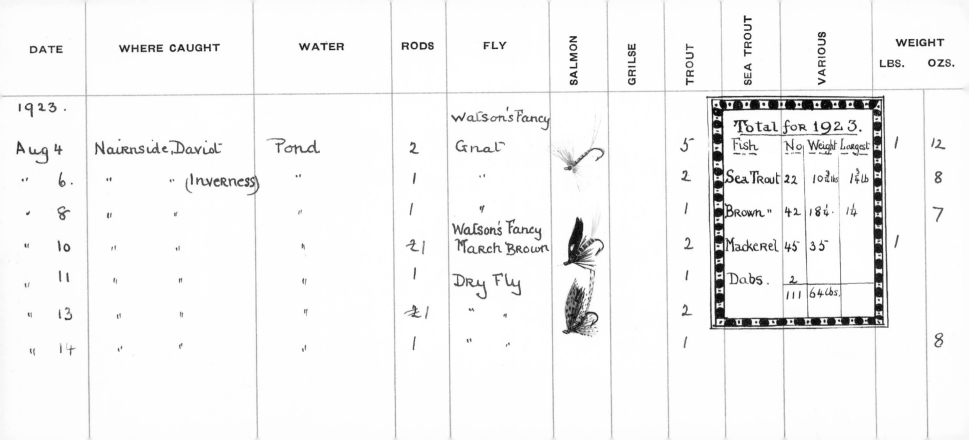

Total for 1923.

Fish	No	Weight	Largest
Sea Trout	22	10¾ lbs	1¾ lb
Brown "	42	18¼	1¼
Mackerel	45	35	
Dabs.	2		
	111	64 lbs.	

Very calm . V.M.B.F. & Self.

Not much breeze.

Very calm .

Fished for a short time

 "   " " "   "

A Nairnside Trout.

DATE	WHERE CAUGHT	WATER	RODS	FLY	SALMON	GRILSE	TROUT	SEA TROUT	VARIOUS	WEIGHT	
										LBS.	OZS.
1924											
May 14	Nairnside, Daviot	Pond	2	March Brown (Dry Fly)			6			1	12
" 15	" " (Inverness	"	1	" "			3			1	4
" 17	" " "	"	1	" "			1				6
" 19	" " "	"	1	Watson's Fancy 4, Olive Dun			4		1		6
" 20	" " "	"	1	Watson's Fancy Coch-y-bondhu Butcher.			3				12
" 22	" " "	"	1	Watson's Fancy			3				14
" 23	" " "	"	1	" "			6			2	12
" 26	" " "	"	1	very small butcher			2				12
May 28 - June 3	Broom R. (Ross)	Sea Pool	1								

Self (4) V.M.B.F. (2)

Saw a stoat take to the water, swim across loch & land almost at my feet.

Dead calm. Very fine tackle. Lost 1 in weeds, hooked another which took cast & flies.

River far too low for salmon. Too early for Sea Trout.

Loch Broom Manse & Church.

DATE	WHERE CAUGHT	WATER	RODS	FLY	SALMON	GRILSE	TROUT	SEA TROUT	VARIOUS	WEIGHT	
										LBS.	OZS.
1924.											
June 6.	Strath Errick, Inverness	Loch Farraline	1				–				
" 7	" " "	" "	2				6			1	8
" 9	" " "	" "	1				5			1	4
" 10	" " "	" "	1				3		Oyster Catcher	3	8
" "	" " "	(Loch of the "Raven") " Bran	1	Minnow (Gold Devon)			2		2 char.	1	4
" 11	Faragaig River	above Torness.	2	small flies			10			2	4
" "	Loch Garth.	Loch Garth	1				–				
" 13	Strath Errick	Loch Farralin	2	various flies			21			5	8
" 14	" "	" "	2	" "			7		Ringed Plover	2	4

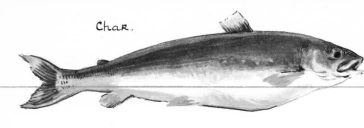

Char.

REMARKS

Dead calm most of time. Hooked & lost a nice fish, my only rise.

From boat, Mr Smith (4) Self (2). Other boat (1) Too calm & bright.

"   "   "   "   (5)   " (0) Fish rising very short. Hooked 2.

Dead calm most of time. Mist low down, heavy showers. Trout on

sunk fly. Char during short spell of sunshine.

Mr Higham (3) Self (7) Threw back about 20 small ones. Fish rising short

Fished for an hour after supper

Mr Smith (12) Self (9) from boat. Wind E. variable. Fish hardly showing

" " (5) " (2) " " Wind W. very strong.

on the shore of
Loch Bran.

DATE	WHERE CAUGHT	WATER	RODS	FLY	SALMON	GRILSE	TROUT	SEA TROUT	VARIOUS	WEIGHT	
										LBS.	OZS.
1924											
June 16	Strath Errick.	Loch Farraline	2	Bloody Butcher			11			3	4
" 17	" "	" "	2	" " Blue Zulu			6			3	
" "	" "	River Courag	2				3				
" 18	" "	Loch Farraline	4				18			3	4
July 8	River Kennet	Newbury Electric Works.	2								
" 9	" "		2								
" 10	Kennet & Avon Canal		2						1 gudgeon		
" 12	R. Kennet & Canal		2								

Bloody Butcher

Blue Zulu

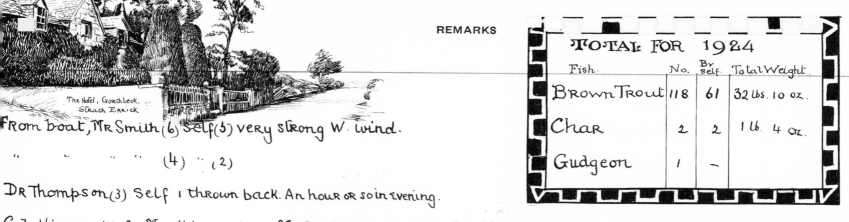

The Hotel, Gorthleck,
Strath Errick

REMARKS

TOTAL FOR 1924			
Fish.	No.	By self.	Total Weight.
Brown Trout	118	61	32 lbs. 10 oz.
Char	2	2	1 lb. 4 oz.
Gudgeon	1	–	

From boat, Mr Smith (6) self (5) very strong W. wind.

"   "   "   " (4) " (2)

Dr Thompson (3) Self 1 thrown back. An hour or so in evening.

Col. Kingscote (3) Mrs Kingscote (4) Mr Smith (6) self (5). Heavy thunderclouds. Fished till 10.45 P.M. 2 boats.

with Ronald. Far too hot & Bright.

"   "   "   "   "   "

R. J. F. (1)   "   "   "   "

A QUIET CORNER OF LOCH BRAN.

DATE	WHERE CAUGHT	WATER	RODS	FLY	SALMON	GRILSE	TROUT	SEA TROUT	VARIOUS	WEIGHT LBS.	WEIGHT OZS.
1925.											
June 10	Black Isle. Ross.	Rosehaugh Loch	2				17			4	12
" 12	Loch Broom Glebe	Loch an Fhiona	2				1				
" 15	" " "	" " L. an Tiompain	2				2				12
" 16	" " "	" an Fhiona	21				2				10
" 18	" " "	" " Tiompain	2				2				9
" "	Loch Broom	near Sea Pool	SWEEP NET						—		
" 19	Loch Broom	" " "	"						3 Flounders	3	12
" "	Loch Broom Glebe.	Loch an Fhiona	1				1				4

Outside "The Hut", Loch Broom.
"Jane", our Neighbour!

Black Throated Diver
on nest. Loch an Phiona.
She always sat with her head
stretched out over the water.

Tom & Violet (1 Rod) (6) Self (11)

1·30 P.M., V.M.B.F. & Self for short time

V.M.B.F. & Self (2) lost 1.

Hooked and lost 2 more.

Self (2) Violet hooked very large Trout

Capt. James", Campbell, Violet, Annie & Self. Wind N.

.. " & " (2) " " " "

9-10 P.M. very cold, N. wind.

Loch Garth, Strath Errick.

DATE	WHERE CAUGHT	WATER	RODS	FLY	SALMON	GRILSE	TROUT	SEA TROUT	VARIOUS	WEIGHT LBS.	WEIGHT OZS.
1925											
June 22	Loch Broom Glebe	Loch a Mhill (L. of the White fairy Knoll)	1	Dry fly			1			2	14
" "	" " "	Loch an Tiompain	3				2			1	2
" 24	" " "	" " "	2	Teal & Red			1				4
" 25	" " "	(Fingal's Loch) Loch an Fhiona	1	Dry Fly (1) Zulu etc			5			1	
" 26	" " "	" " "	1	March Brown			1				4
" 27	" " "	Loch an Tiompain	2	Dry Fly .			2			1	
" 29	" " "	Loch a Mhill	1	Sea Trout fly.			1			3	
" 30	" " "	Loch an Tiompain	2	Dry Fly etc .			5			2	8

Golden Plover chick.

Wigeon on
Loch an Tiompain.

Cast tapered to 3X. Fish 18½"

V.M.B.F (1) Annie Sutherland 7self.(1) Turning, from boat.

Self (1) Violet 7 Colin.

Cold 7 misty. Wind N.

"   "   "   "   "

N.E. Wind. self (2) Annie lost a nice fish. From Boat.

It (and J!) Ran ¾ length of loch, without stopping.

Turned very wet. Annie (1) self (4) largest 1lb; two

when trolling a fly.

The End of the Day.

DATE	WHERE CAUGHT	WATER	RODS	FLY	SALMON	GRILSE	TROUT	SEA TROUT	VARIOUS	WEIGHT	
										LBS.	OZS.
1925											
July 2	Strath Errick	River Courag	1	Dry Fly.			1				4
" "	" " (Inverness)	Loch Farraline	1	Zulu etc.			7			4	2
July 3	" "	River Courag	1	Dry Fly			4				13
" "	" "	Loch Farraline	1	Teal & Black			1				4
" 4	" "	Loch Bran	1	Dry Fly			1				
" "	" "	Courag R.	1	small March Brown			2				9
" "	" "	Loch Farraline	1	Teal & Black			2				12
" 6	" "	River Courag.	1	Dry Fly (5)			8			1	12
"											

Zulu

Teal & Black

March Brown

Red Breasted Merganser.

Too bright. River very low.

Fished 8-11 P.M. R. Largest fish 2 lbs.

Too calm nothing doing

Too calm

8-10 P.M. Caught stickleback on big Claret & Grouse.

Threw back several small.

Loch Farraline, Strath Errick.

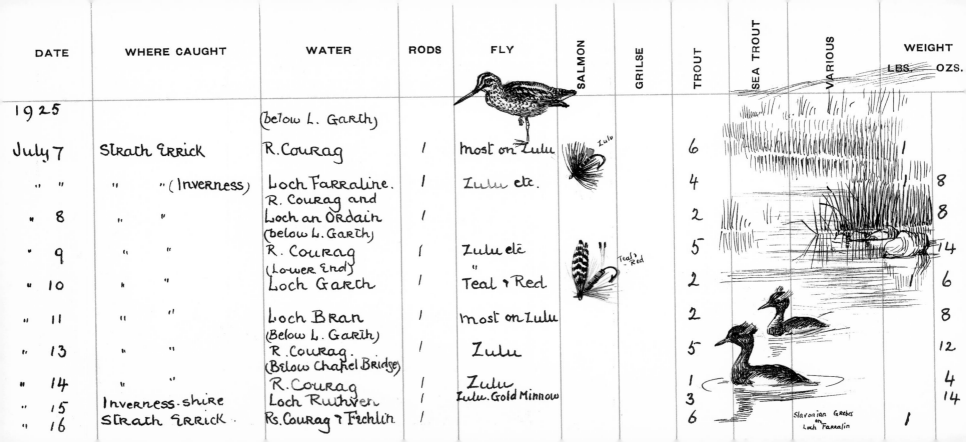

DATE	WHERE CAUGHT	WATER	RODS	FLY	SALMON	GRILSE	TROUT	SEA TROUT	VARIOUS	WEIGHT LBS.	OZS.
1925		(below L. Garth)									
July 7	Strath Errick	R. Courag	1	Most on Zulu			6				1
" "	" " (Inverness)	Loch Farraline.	1	Zulu etc.			4				8
" 8	" "	R. Courag and Loch an Ordain	1				2				8
" 9	" "	(below L. Garth) R. Courag	1	Zulu etc "			5				14
" 10	" "	(Lower End) Loch Garth	1	Teal & Red			2				6
" 11	" "	Loch Bran	1	Most on Zulu			2				8
" 13	" "	(Below L. Garth) R. Courag.	1	Zulu			5				12
" 14	" "	(Below Chapel Bridge) R. Courag	1	Zulu Zulu. Gold Minnow			1				4
" 15	Inverness. shire	Loch Ruthven	1				3				14
" 16	Strath Errick .	Rs. Courag & Fechlin	1				6				1

Zulu

Teal & Red

Slavonian Grebes on Loch Farralin

Raven
(Loch Ruthven.)

Rising short. Threw back several. 2 on 1 cast.

Very cold – Fished 8–10 P.M.

Difficult loch to fish from bank. Very boggy.

Threw back 6 even smaller.

Saw no other Rises.

Threw back 4 more.

Fished for ½ hr.

Threw 1 back, another broke my minnow

Threw 1 back.

TOTAL FOR 1925			
		by self.	
Brown Trout	105	97	36 ¼ lbs
Flounders	3	(in net)	3 ¾ lbs.
	108	97	40 lbs

Largest Trout, 3 lbs; 2 lbs. 14 oz.; 2 lbs.; 1 lb. 3 oz..

DATE	WHERE CAUGHT	WATER	RODS	FLY	SALMON	GRILSE	TROUT	SEA TROUT	VARIOUS	WEIGHT	
										LBS.	OZS.
1926.				Small Silver Doctor (most)							
June 14	Dundonnell. Ross.	Loch na h'airbhe	1	Zulu			15			2	2
" 15	"	Logie Loch	1	small silver Doctor (most) Zulu.			6			2	2
,, 16	"	L. a Bhaid-choille	1	most on small silver Doctor, Zulu			19			4	8
" 17	"	Glebe Lochs	1				-				
" 18	" (Faighn)	Heather Lochs	1	most on Variant			15			5	0
" "	"	L. a Bhaid-choille	1	"			5			1	
" 19		" " "	1	Dark Partridge			5			1	
" "	Little Loch Broom		1	Spoon					2 coal fish	18	8

Ring Ousel

Black Throated Diver

VARIANT

Partridge.

Only small trout in loch.

One was exactly like a sea trout.

Threw back 7 more - small -

Too bright & hot enough wind E.

Very hot & bright

9-10 P.M. glorious evening.

Fished for 2 hrs. in the rain.

Wet & stormy.

DATE	WHERE CAUGHT	WATER	RODS	FLY	SALMON	GRILSE	TROUT	SEA TROUT	VARIOUS	WEIGHT LBS.	OZS.
1926											
June 21	Dundonnell. Ross	Logie Loch	1	Dark Partridge			6	3		1	8
" 22	" "	" "	1	" "				2			5
" 23	" "	" "	1	Zulu			1				8
" 24	" "	Off Kildonan Rocks (G. Aird-easaidh = Promontory of the Fall Stream.)	2	Natural Minnow				1	1 lythe 3 coal fish	18	2
" 25	" "	Ardessie Burn	1	(Worm) Dark Partridge			7				1
" 26	" "	L. a Bhaid-choille	2	Zulu			9				2
" "	Little Loch Broom		1	Red eel			~~8~~		8 coal fish	7	4
" 28	" " "		1	Eels and Spoons			~~28~~		28 " "	252	
" "											

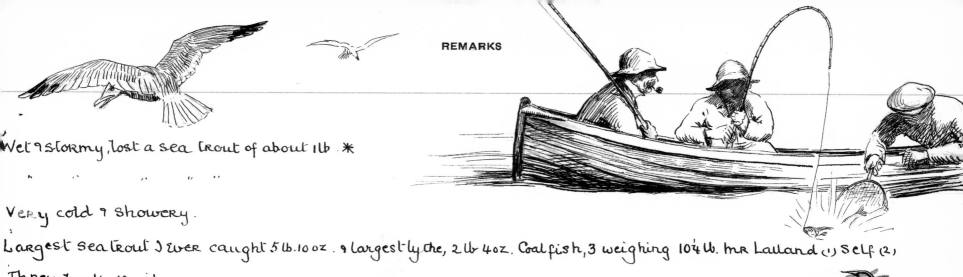

Wet & stormy, lost a sea trout of about 1lb. *

"   "   "   "   "

Very cold & showery.

Largest sea trout I ever caught 5 lb. 10 oz. & largest by the, 2 lb 4 oz. Coal fish, 3 weighing 10¼ lb. Mr Lalland (1) Self (2)

Threw back 12. *

Tom Ferguson (fishing for an hour) (1) Self (8)

4 of 10 lbs each, 2 of 9 lbs, 2 of 8 lbs. Other boat 11 fish, 100 lbs.

Fished from 10 till 2 P.M.

Spoon

* It is a difficult problem as to how the Logie Loch sea trout came to be there. Whether (1) They are brown trout, though silvery like
fresh run sea trout & with scales easily rubbing off. They play like sea trout, quite unlike the Brown trout in the loch (2) they are
descended from sea trout caught as fry in the burns & put into the loch, or whether (3) They are really fresh run sea trout, having
got up an, apparently, inaccessible burn. Sea trout are found at the bottom of this burn, near the River. It is nearest burn to sea

DATE	WHERE CAUGHT	WATER	RODS	FLY	SALMON	GRILSE	TROUT	SEA TROUT	Rainbow Trout	VARIOUS	WEIGHT LBS.	OZS.
1926.		(Loch na Liagaidh = Loch of the place of The hollow)										
June 28	Dundonnell. Ross.	Logie Loch	1	Butcher		Partridge	1	1			1	2
July 2	R. Granta. Cambs.	Below Gates at	1	Dark Partridge						1		
„ 3		Hildersham	1				—					
„ 4		„	1			Butcher	3			1		
„ 5	„	above gates	1	Dry Fly			1					
„ 7	„		1	„ and Alexandra		Alexandra,	2			3	about	12
„ 8	„	Below gates	1			Alexandra.	1			1	„ 1	
„ 9	„						1			^		
„ 10	„			Dark Partridge						2		

Fished for 1½ hrs. in evening.

Small. 12" limit on this River

Lost a fish of 1lb. Cast wound Round submerged branch

under the limit, 2 small & 2 about 1½ lb. together.

With O.B.F.

DATE	WHERE CAUGHT	WATER	RODS	FLY	SALMON	GRILSE	TROUT	SEA TROUT	Rainbow Trout / VARIOUS	WEIGHT LBS.	OZS.
1926											
July 11	R. Granta . Cambs.		1						1		
„ 13	„		1	Red Palmer					4		
„ 14	„	Hildersham.	1	„ „ „			1				12
„ 15	„	Pembroke Fishing Club. (Linton . above & below)	1	Butcher			2		2		
„ 16	„			Red Tag, Palmer			1		2		
„ 17	„			Red Palmer			1		2	about	
„ 18	„			„ „			1		5	1	1
„ 19	„	Pembroke Fishing Club above Linton & Hildersham .		Red Palmer			2		2	1	
„ 20	„			Alexandra			5		4	1	8

With O.B.F.

Osborn (12) Orby Clifford (3) Self (6)

O.B.F. (7) Self (4)

Largest Trout 1lb 13oz (16½")

River Granta above the Weir
Hildersham

DATE	WHERE CAUGHT	WATER	RODS	FLY	SALMON	GRILSE	TROUT	SEA TROUT	Rainbow Trout	VARIOUS	WEIGHT	
											LBS.	OZS.
1926				Alexandra.		Teal ? Silver.						
July 21	R. Granta. Cambs.	Below the Weir								1		
" 22		Below the Gates		Teal & Silver			2			1		
" 24		" " "								1	1	8

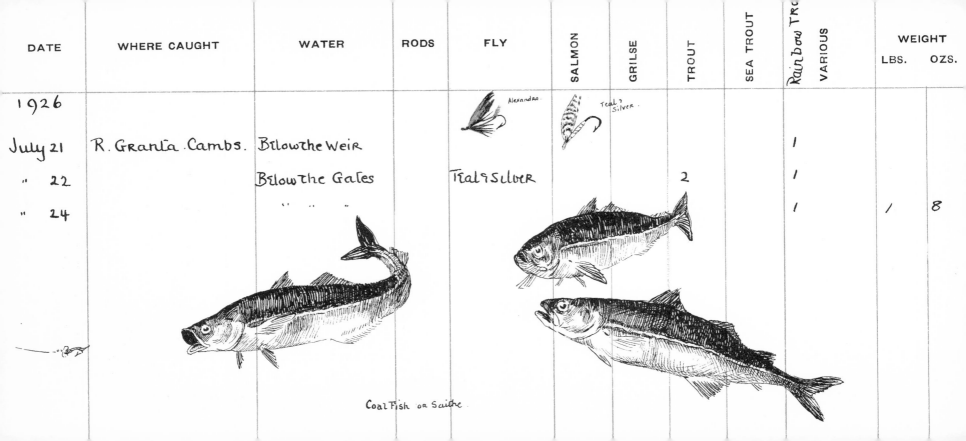

Coal Fish or Saithe.

REMARKS

River too muddy after storm.

Largest Brown Trout 1 lb. 2 oz.

During July, O.B.F. caught 62, self 56.

Rainbow & Brown Trout.

TOTAL FOR 1926

Fish	No.	Weight lbs.	oz	Largest
Brown Trout	111	26	13	1 lb. 13 oz.
Rainbow "	33	6	8	10 oz.
Sea "	8	8	6	5 lbs. 10 oz
Coal Fish (Saithe)	41	354	12	10 lbs
Pollack (Lythe)	1	2	4	2¼ lbs
	194	398	11	

DATE	WHERE CAUGHT	WATER	RODS	FLY	SALMON	GRILSE	TROUT	SEA TROUT	Rainbow Trout / VARIOUS	WEIGHT LBS.	OZS.
1927											
May 17	Lambourn R. BERKS	Newbury Angling Association	2				—				
„ 18	„ 9 Kennet Rs.	„	2				1				4
„ 19	„ River	„	2				2				
„ 23	„ „	„	2				1				
„ 25	River Granta	Hildersham, below	1				32		1		8
„ 26	„ „ Cambs	gates (most)	1	Tinsel Flies			5		3	2	1
„ 27	„ „ „	„ 9 about Weir	1	„ very small Teal & silver			3		1	1	1
„ 28	„ „ „	Pool & stream below	1	Alexandra			1		1		10
„ 30	„ „ „	„	1	Bloody Mary			1				2

LAMBOURN RIVER

Orange Tip

With Ronald.

R.J.F. & self.

Both by R.T.F

Fish only splashing at fly.

VERY cold. N.E.

DATE	WHERE CAUGHT	WATER	RODS	FLY	SALMON	GRILSE	TROUT	SEA TROUT	VARIOUS	WEIGHT	
										LBS.	OZS.
1927											
May 31	R. Granta. Cambs.	Below the Granary Bridge.	1	Red Quill			2				8
June 3	Faragaig R. Inverness	1mile above Torness	1	Zulu			23			5	8
" 4	Strath Errick.	Loch Farralin	1	Coch-y-bondhu			10			3	8
" 6	" "	" "	1	Zulu " olive Dun 1 on Dry Fly			11			3	4
" 7	" "	" "	1	Zulu Zulu (4) Butcher (1)			12			4	2
" 8	Inverness-shire	" Ruthven	1	Nymph (1) Minnow (2) Coch-y-bondhu.			10			4	
" 9	Strath Errick	" an Ordain	1	Zulu Alexandra			23			4	12
" 10	" "	" an Urigh. "Mystery Loch"	1	Zulu Teal & Red			3			2	2
" 11	" "	Faragaig River	2	Zulu			10			1	12

Slavonian Grebe on Loch Farralin

Jack Snipe.

Loch Farraline by moonlight.

of $\frac{3}{4}$ lb each. Threw back a lot of the small ones

Wind W. very cold & squally, fish rising short.

John Cameron - ghillie - June 4 -15 -

" " " Self (11) Miss McGillivray (1)

Wind variable. Fish rising very short. Largest $\frac{3}{4}$ lb.

Very cold. Hail storm. Largest $\frac{3}{4}$ lb.

Cold day. Best fish, 1 lb., $\frac{3}{4}$ lb; Lost 3 very good fish.

Miss Mc. Gillivray (2) self (8) Largest 14 oz. Threw back small fish.

DATE	WHERE CAUGHT	WATER	RODS	FLY	SALMON	GRILSE	TROUT	SEA TROUT	VARIOUS	LBS.	OZS.
1927				most on					Wigeon		
June 13	Dell Forest . Inverness.	Loch Kemp.	1	Teal & Red Minnow, 4 on			19			3	8
" 14	Strath Errick. "	Loch Farraline	1	silver 1 on blue Silver Minnow (3)			5			2	8
" 15	" "	" "	1	Zulu, Nymph (3)			10			2	8
" 20	Eastbourne. Sussex	(Pier Below Wish Tower	3	Lug Worm			12		12 dabs		
" 21	" "	From Pier	9	Rag Worm			4		5-4 {8 dabs, 1 Bass, 1 Crab	1	
July 11	River Granta . Camb.	In 9 below Pool Pembroke Fishing club.	2	Coch y bondhu			1		2 Rainbow Trout	1	8
" 12	" " "	Above Linton	2	Alder			1				10
" 13	" " "	Below Weir . Pembroke Fishing Club	2	Badger Hackle			1				4
" 14	" " "	Abington Hall	2	Badger Hackle			1		1 Rainbow Trout		8

A lot of small fish rising short.

Not taking the fly well. Largest $\frac{3}{4}$ lb.

Ronald (2) Boatman (2) Self (8)

" (2 dabs) Self Bass of 1 lb. 1 crab.

R.T.F. (2) Self 1 Rainbow of $\frac{1}{2}$ lb

" (2) Self (1) of 10 oz.

" (2) 1 Rainbow 1 1 brown.

Self (1) Ronald (2)

DATE	WHERE CAUGHT	WATER	RODS	FLY	SALMON	GRILSE	TROUT	SEA TROUT	Rainbow Trout	VARIOUS	WEIGHT LBS.	OZS.
1927		Pembroke Fishing Club;										
July 15	River Granta.	above Linton	2				—					
" 18		Below Gates	1				3			2	1	
" 19		Above Weir	1				1			1		6
" 21		" "	1				1					3
" 22		" "	1							1		3
Aug. 16	Lambourn R. Berks.	Piscatorial Society Maj. Nightingale (member)	1				2					8
" 17	" "	N.A.A. Water.	1				1					5
" 18	" "	" " " "	1				1					7
" 19	" "	" " " "	1				—					
Nov.	" "	" " " "	2									

The Little Owl that lived in the big Willow.

A Poem

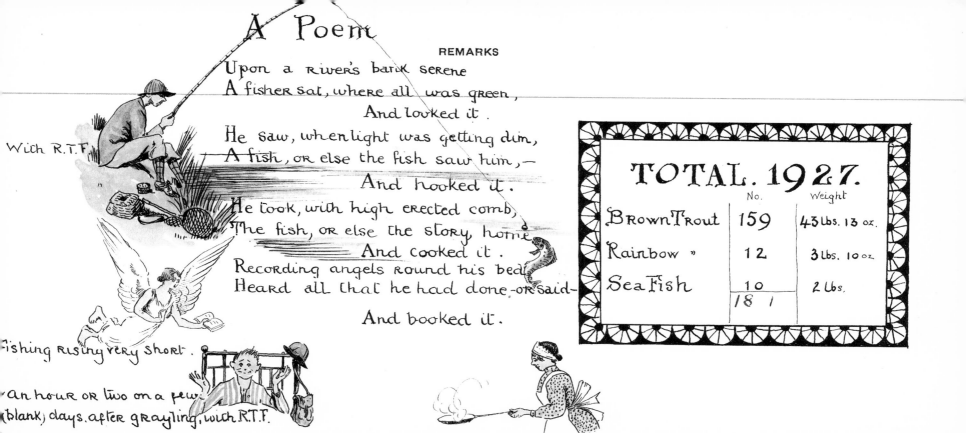

Upon a river's bank serene
A fisher sat, where all was green,
      And looked it.
He saw, when light was getting dim,
A fish, or else the fish saw him,—
      And hooked it.
He took, with high erected comb,
The fish, or else the story, home
      And cooked it.
Recording angels round his bed
Heard all that he had done or said—
      And booked it.

With R.T.F.

Fishing rising very short.

An hour or two on a few (blank) days. after grayling, with R.T.F.

TOTAL. 1927.	No.	Weight
Brown Trout	159	43 lbs. 13 oz.
Rainbow "	12	3 lbs. 10 oz.
Sea Fish	10	2 lbs.
	181	

DATE	WHERE CAUGHT	WATER	RODS	FLY	SALMON	GRILSE	TROUT	SEA TROUT	VARIOUS	WEIGHT LBS.	OZS.
1928											
May 1.	River Granta. Cambs	Pool below Gates	1	Red Tag					1 Rainbow Trout		14
" 2	" , "	"	1	Large gold. ribbed Hares ear			2		1 " "	1	2
" 6	" " "	"	1	Red Tag			3				18
" 8	" " "	"	1				1				84
June 15	Milford. Co. Donegal	Lough Columbkille	1				-				
" 16	" " "	" Fern	1				-				
" 18		" "	1				8				
" 19		" "	1	Pheasant Tail			9				
" 20		" "	1				1				

Rainbow Trout

Arrived here this evening to camp

in empty house for a week. N. to N.E.
Heavy thunderstorm made river
muddy & unfishable for 3 days.

First visit to Ireland. Fished 2 hours.

Too bright "A Black Day, sure enough!"

Dennis Sweeney - ghillie - for 3 weeks.

Threw back 42.

Rose a salmon. Threw back the Trout.

Salmon Rising in
Lough Fern

DATE	WHERE CAUGHT	WATER	RODS	FLY	SALMON	GRILSE	TROUT	SEA TROUT	VARIOUS	WEIGHT LBS.	OZS.
1928											
June 21	Co. Donegal. Ireland	Lough FERN Lochs Dhu and	1	Bloody Butcher			1		Cormorant on Lough Fern.		
" 22	" " "	Columbkille.	1				—				
" 23	" " "	" 9 Dhu	1				3				
" 24	" " "	" 9 Dhu	2				—				
" 25	" " "	Lough FERN	1	March Brown			7			1	4
" 26	" " "	" " and	1	" " (17)	—		21			5	
" 27	" " "	Lennan River (2 hools above lough)	1	" " (3)	—		5			1	
" 28	" " "	L. FERN 9 Lennan R (above Kilmacrennan)	1	" "	—		2				8
" 29	" " "	Lennan R.		Fiery Brown	—						

Fly illustrations: Bloody Butcher, Fiery Brown, Fiery Brown (Irish Pattern), March Brown

R.T.F. y M.C.F. on
Lough Dhu.

Great Crested Grebes
on Lough Fern.

ose a salmon. Threw back the trout.

igh wind. Fearfully squally. 1lb limit on L. Columbkille, famous for very heavy trout.

qually. Hooked & lost a very heavy trout, rose another on Loch.C. Caught 2 of ½lb each on one cast on Loch Dhu.

.T.F. & self. Did not fish very seriously.

lenty of salmon rising, but not to fly.

Rose what both Dennis & J thought was a salmon on small March Brown

Rose a salmon. A good many boats out every day but very few fish caught, though many showing

lenty of salmon rising but will not take fly. Wind S.

Rose 1 fish. S. Gale. 7 Rods, no fish.

DATE	WHERE CAUGHT	WATER	RODS	FLY	SALMON	GRILSE	TROUT	SEA TROUT	VARIOUS	WEIGHT LBS.	OZS.
1928		Lennan River									
June 30	Co. Donegal. Ireland	above Kilmacrennan (Black Loch)	1	Fiery Brown	—						
July 2	Co. Donegal, "	Lough Dhu.	1				1				10
" 3	" " "	" Fern & Lennan River	1				2				6
" "	" " "	Lough Columbkille	1	Teal, Red & Silver (small)			3			1	10
" 4	" " "	Lennan River & Lough Fern	1	March Brown	—		1				
" 5	" " "	Lennan R. (above Kilmacrennan) Lough Fern	1	March Brown	—		4				12

Fiery Brown (Irish Pattern)

Teal Red & Silver

March Brown.

REMARKS

Carrying home the peats.

ose 1 salmon, Wind S. River in good order. 9 rods, no fish

earful S.W. Gale, very squally. Hardly could keep fly on water. Hopeless for trout fishing

Lot of salmon rising but would not take. Wind changed & loch became muddy & unfishable.

ished from 8 P.M. — 12.30 A.M. No wind. Big rise of heavy trout. 1 of 1½ lbs. threw back 2 (1 lb. limit)

looked & lost a salmon in the lough, while fishing for trout with 4x cast & trout flies. Played him 5 — 10 minutes, then

he ran out a lot of line then jumped & was off. Rose another in the Crana Pool on River.

Rose 2 salmon on trout fly A most disappointing season, the worst on record, though there is a

record number of fish up A great many fish showing but not taking the fly, even when casting

over a good head & tail rise.

DATE	WHERE CAUGHT	WATER	RODS	FLY	SALMON	GRILSE	TROUT	SEA TROUT	VARIOUS	WEIGHT	
										LBS.	OZS
1928	Londonderry. Ireland.										
July 6	R. ~~Granta~~ Cambs	Faughan R.	2	March Brown			6				
" 7	"	Burndennet	2				30			verysma	
" 8	"	Burntollet	3				63			"	.
Aug. 1	R. Granta Cambs.	R. Granta. Cambs.	1				-				
" 2		Below gates	1				1			1	
" 3		"	1				2			1	
" 4		"	1				1		1 Rainbow T.		12
" 6		Pembroke Fishing Club Abingdon	1				2				8
Nov. 5	R. Lambourn.	Newbury Angling As.	2				Grayling				

R.T.T. (4) Self (2)

   " (23) " (7)

   " (32) " (24) Col. Dumbell (7)

O.B.T. (1) 1 lb.

Lost 2 Rainbows, 1 after its 6th jump.

O R by Clifford. 1 Rainbow ¾ lb.

T.F. 9 self. River too low.

REMARKS

Hildersham - Old Mill House from across the Pool.

DATE	WHERE CAUGHT	WATER	RODS	FLY	SALMON	GRILSE	TROUT	SEA TROUT	VARIOUS	WEIGHT	
										LBS.	OZS.
1928.						Grayling					
Nov. 9.º	River Kennet	Hungerford Fishery	2	Orange Tag.	Orange Tag	—	3 (Close season, threw back.			1	4
Nov. 12	Lambourn River.	Newbury Angling Ass!	2	" "		1	3 "	"	" "		
1929											
Feb. 9	Folkestone	Railway Pier	2 lines	Dungeness Lug				—			
May 8	Lough Corn. Co. Mayo	South end	1	Claret & Mallard							
" 9	" " " "		1	Minnow (!)			3			1	12
" 10	" " " "	Off Illannaglashy	1	Woodcock & claret			1				4
" 11	" " "		1	Minnow ("Natural Bait" Minnow)			8			5	
							12			7 lbs.	

Grayling

REMARKS

Grayling

R.T.F. (1) self (2) 12" & 9". N.E.

.T.F. (3) self. (1) My first Grayling.

R.T.F. & self Fishing for 2 hours.

For 2 hours on arrival. Cold. N.

Cold. W. Threw back small one. Rain all night.

Cold S.W. Nothing doing.

Largest 1¾ lb.   Boatman, Jimmy Burke.

Fish	No	Weight	Heaviest
Brown Trout	108	24 lbs (about)	1 lb. 4 oz
Rainbow "	2	1 lb 5 oz	14 oz
Grayling	1		

TOTAL FOR 1928.

DATE	WHERE CAUGHT	WATER	RODS	FLY	SALMON	GRILSE	TROUT	SEA TROUT	VARIOUS	WEIGHT LBS.	OZS.
1929				"Natural Bait" Minnow.	Brought forward 12					7 {1	4
May 13	Lough Conn. Co. Mayo.	Pontoon End.	1	Brown Devon Minnow (pike)			2		1 Pike	14	
May 14	Lough Conn.	" "	1	Minnow			4			6	8
" "	Lough Cullen	Below Pontoon Bridge	1	Spoon	1				1 Pike.	28	
May 15	Loughs Conn & Cullen			Natural Bait Minnow .							
May 16.	Lough Conn						1				8
May 17	Loughs Conn & Cullen.			Same minnow Spoon (pike)			1		1 Pike	5	8
May 18	Lough Conn	Six Arch Bay (most)		Silver Devon			7			7	8
					1		2 7		3	70	4/4

up to date 27 trout weighing 23 lbs.

(Alcocks "Natural Bait")

S. Gale. Had to pull up boat in a sheltered bay & walk home.

Largest 3¾ lbs; 1¾ lbs. Wind very high N.W. used big boat & two men. Too stormy to start till after lunch.

Salmon 21 lbs; pike 7 lbs. Best day's fishing I ever had! Played salmon about ¾ hour.

Wind N. Never had a rise. Cullen too dirty, loughs rising very fast. Cullen flowing into Conn. 1st Mayfly.

Wind S. a few trout rose short to the fly. Saw over 20 Mayfly on Cullen. Conn & Cullen even today.

Pike 5¼ lbs in Cullen. Conn flowing into Cullen.

Largest trout a 3¼ lb. gillaroo; 1½ lb; 1 lb. Lost the fish of my life. Saw him jump out of the water thought it was a grilse — trolled over him & hooked him. He ran out a tremendous lot of line, came up & lashed on the surface & took my minnow! Jimmy thought him an 8 pounder!

broke me

DATE	WHERE CAUGHT	WATER	RODS	FLY	SALMON	GRILSE	TROUT	SEA TROUT	VARIOUS	WEIGHT	
										LBS.	OZS.

REMARKS

DATE	WHERE CAUGHT	WATER	RODS	FLY	SALMON	GRILSE	TROUT	SEA TROUT	VARIOUS	WEIGHT LBS.	OZS.
	— Brought Forward —	6 Arch Bay etc. (Hotel Bay (pike)		pike on Silver Devon.	1		27		3 pike	70	4
May 20	Lough Conn	Hotel Bay (pike)		Small minnow			6		1 Pike.	20	
May 21	" "	Schoolhouse Bay		Silver Devon			1				8
May 22	Lough Cullen			Dapping			3			3	
May 23	Loughs Conn & Cullen	Six Arch Bay		Dapping			4			2	4
May 24	Lough Conn	Six Arch Bay		Dapping			8			4	4
May 25	" "	Bilberry Bay Six Arch Bay	2	Dapping			6			5	
May 28?	" "	Six Arch Bay		Dapping			8			4	
May 29	" "			Dapping			4			1	12
May 29	" Cullen.			Dapping			1				13/12

Total for 3 weeks. 1 salmon, 21 lbs, 4 pike (16 lbs,14 ub. 7 lb. 5·4) 64 trout weighing 51¼ lbs.   4 pike   111   12

Pike

Whimbrel

REMARKS

Pike 16 lbs. Dead calm & very hot most of day.

Nothing doing. Very stormy later. S.

Wet and beastly. Plenty of May fly.

Too much wind on Cullen, not much fly on Conn.

No rise of fly on Conn. Picked up flies on Cullen.

Mrs St John (4) Self (2) 1½ lbs; ¼ lb put back.

Largest 2¾ lbs.

Much too hot & bright. Wind variable.

Too bright. Fished 3 hours before leaving

DATE	WHERE CAUGHT	WATER	RODS	FLY	SALMON	GRILSE	TROUT	SEA TROUT	VARIOUS	WEIGHT LBS.	OZS.
1929											
June 25	River Kennet & Kennet & Avon Canal	N.A.A.	2								
June 26.	Kennet, Lambourn & Canal	N.A.A.	1								
June 27.	Rivers Kennet & Lambourn	N.A.A.									
July 11	River Granta	Grantchester Mill.	2								
July 17		Hildersham Mill	2					1			12.
July 19		Below the gates	2.	Red Tag (3) Minnow			4.			1	8
July 21		Below 2nd Weir	2	Red Tag.			1				
July 23		Below gates	1	Variant			1				4
July 27	" "	Granary Reach.	1	Variant			—				

"THE SWAN". NEWBURY

REMARKS

KENNET & AVON CANAL.

with Mrs Mitchell. We did not fish much but she showed me the best spots on the club & free waters from below Bull's Lock to above Newbury.

Much too hot & bright.

Weed cutting on both RIVERS. The last Mayfly!

Coarse fishing with Bunk Clifford, 2 gudgeon by him.

On oRange Tag. With O.B.F. Intensely hot. Very few fish being caught during this drought.

Self 2. 1 BROWN TROUT 1lb, Rainbow 6oz. O.B.F. 2 below 2nd WEIR. (Greenhouse Pool)

O.B.F. Self none, - a few Rises -

Rainbow Trout.

Lost a trout of 1lb. under the trees.

VARIANT.

DATE	WHERE CAUGHT	WATER	RODS	FLY	SALMON	GRILSE	TROUT	SEA TROUT	VARIOUS	WEIGHT LBS.	OZS.
1929		Pembroke Fishing Club, above Linton.									
July 30	River Granta	The Pool. Hildersham	2	Minnow			1				12
Aug. 19	River Kennet	Below Bull's Lock (NAA)	1								
Aug. 20.	" "	" " "	2								
Aug 21	River Lambourn	Below Railway Bridge	1	Variant				1			
Aug 22	Rs. Kennet & Lambourn	Below Bull's Lock.	1	Variant							
Aug 23	River Kennet & Avon C.	Below Ham Lock.	1								
Nov. 25	Folkestone	Railway Pier	2	Black lug.							

Total for 1929

	No.	Weight	Heaviest Fish	
Salmon	1	21 lbs	21 lbs	
Trout	68	54 lbs.	3¾ lb, 3¼, 2¼	
Rainbow	2	16 oz		1 gudgeon!
Pike	4	42 lbs 4 oz	16 lbs. 14 lbs.	1 crab.
Sundries	1			
	76	118 lbs		

The Lambourn below Shaw

River very full of weeds above Linton, nothing doing

Tried for the very big trout with a minnow, no luck

In the Evening - a few coarse fish Rising.

With Mrs Mitchell - a few chub & dace Rising.

mall trout Rising short on Lambourn in evening.

Trying for Roach & perch, no luck at all.

R.J.F. & self. for an hour.

The House on the Hill.

DATE	WHERE CAUGHT	WATER	RODS	FLY	SALMON	GRILSE	TROUT	SEA TROUT	VARIOUS	WEIGHT LBS.	OZS.
1930											
May 30	L. Cullen. Co. Mayo		1				—				
May 31	L. Cullen.		1	Dapping &			2			1	8
June 2.	Lough Cullen.		1	" Minnow.			1	1	1 pike	6	0
" 3	Lough Conn	Six Arch Bay	1	Dapping & Minnow (6)			12		2 perch	6	0
" 4	" "	" " "	1	Dapping & Minnow (5)			7		3 "	5	0
" 5	" "	" " "	1	"			0				
" 6	" "	" " "	1	"			8			3	4
" 7	" "	" " "	1	Dapping			10			4	8
							40	1	6	26	4

Alcock's "TRUE FORM"

REMARKS

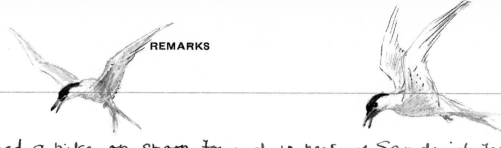

S.E. Too calm & thundery. Touched a pike on spoon. Found 12 nests of Sandwich Tern on Grippen Island

N.W. to S.E. thundery, lost 1 fish on dap & 2 on minnow. Largest 1¼ lbs. Jimmy Burke, boatman.

Pike 5½ lbs.

Largest trout 1¼ lbs, 1 lb. 1 lb. Very hot.

Largest trout 1 lb. 6 oz gillaroo. Too calm & very hot. Found 9 nests of Com. Tern on an island.

Wind very variable, Fish Rising very short. Very hot day.

Strong N. wind. mostly small fish showing, all Rising very short.

Largest 1 lb 6 oz. gillaroo. Wind N. Found 2 nests of Tufted Duck, 3 of Merganser, 1 g Mallard & 1 g Reed Bunt.

DATE	WHERE CAUGHT	WATER	RODS	FLY	SALMON	GRILSE	TROUT	SEA TROUT	VARIOUS	WEIGHT LBS.	OZS.
1930.	Brought forward						40	1	6	26	4
June 8	Lough Conn	Six Arch Bay	1	Dapping			4			2	8
June 9	" "	Six Arch Bay & House Bay	1	Dapping & Minnow (3)			7			2	12
June 10	" "	Off Glass Island	1	Dapping & Minnow (1)			4			4	4
June 11	" "	Six Arch Bay & House Bay	1	Dapping			5			2	
June 12	" "	off Glass Island & S.E. shore	1	"			7			9	
June 13	" "	S.E. Shore	1	Dapping Minnow (1)			6			5	12
June 14	" "	S.E. Shore & KnocMore Bay	1	Dapping			7			7	0
	up to date 80 trout weighing 52½ lbs						80	1	6	59	8

REMARKS

A Gillaroo

Wind S.W. to W. only went out after lunch.

Wind W. strong. Rain all day

Largest 2¼ lb. gillaroo. Squally & stormy, wind W.

Wind W. stormy & very squally.

2 gillaroo, 3½ lbs (22") 2½ lbs (20") 1¼ lb. Biggest fish in boat in 3 minutes. a Tern picked up my fly, then dropped it.

Wind S. to W. Broke the blowline, caught it in the water, played the fish on it, it broke again & picked up by Jimmy, & we got the fish ~ 1lb ~. Best trout 1 lb. 7 ozs; 1½ lb. 1¼ lbs. 1 lb.

Gillaroo 2¾ lb. other trout 1¾ lbs. 1 lb. Wind S. (Length of gillaroo, 19")

DATE	WHERE CAUGHT	WATER	RODS	FLY	SALMON	GRILSE	TROUT	SEA TROUT	VARIOUS	WEIGHT LBS.	OZS.
1930	Brought forward —						80	1	6	59	8
June 15	Lough Conn	off Glass Island	1	1 on Minnow 2 on dap.			3			4	12
July 7	R. Granta, Hildersham.	Below 3rd Weir The Pool.	1								
July 8	" "		1								
July 9		Below 1st Weir The Pool.	1								
July 10		Below 2nd Weir The Pool.	1								
July 11			1								
July 12		(2) The Pool Pembroke Fishing	1								
July 13		(1) Club. Abington	1				83	1	6	64	4

REMARKS

Gillaroo 3½ lbs. Played him to the net in 1 minute. Only went out at 4 o'clk.

Rose 5 - short. River very low after long drought.

Thundery. Saw a good fish in the Pool.

Rose 2 - short. Otter hounds came round, picked up scent of otter at head end of pool, fresh tracks ∧

Rose 2, still rising short. Very thundery. Rose a good fish in the Pool, very small below Weir.

Very cold. N.E.

N to NE. cold & overcast. Hooked and lost one below Hall. Rose 2 others. Hall water very low & choked with weeds.

Rose 1 in the Pool.

higher up the River

Ireland		
83	trout	57¼ lbs.
1	sea trout	¼ "
5	perch	1¼ "
1	pike	5½ "
90		64¼ lbs.

DATE	WHERE CAUGHT	WATER	RODS	FLY	SALMON	GRILSE	TROUT	SEA TROUT	VARIOUS	WEIGHT LBS.	OZS.
1930											
	Brought forward						80	1	6	64	4
Oct. 2	R. Lambourn.	N.A.A. Water	1						—		
" 3	" "	" "	2						—		
" 6	Kennet & Avon Canal	Below Hatts Lock	2	—					—		
" 8	River Kennet	Below Bull's Lock	1	Minnow on shadow fly tied by Miss Freeman of Hungerford.			(thrown back) 1				
" 11	R. Lambourn.	N.A.A. Water	2						3 grayling		
Nov. 4	" "	" " "	2						—		
" 5	Kennet & Canal.	Below Bull's Lock.	1								
" 6	" "	" " "	1				81	1	9	65	

Green sandpiper

Water Rail

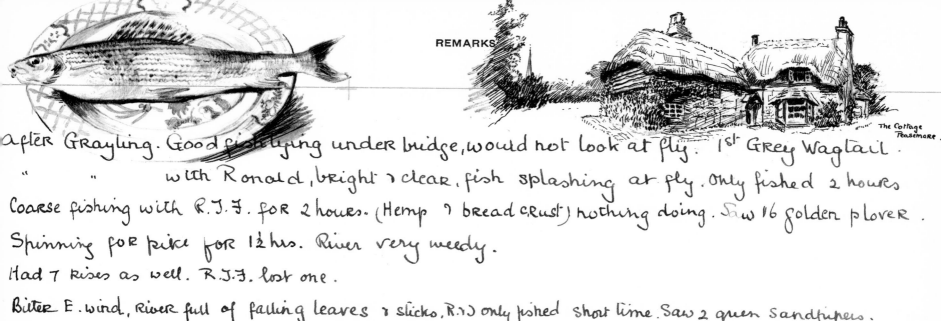

The Cottage
Peasemore.

After Grayling. Good fishing under bridge, would not look at fly. 1st Grey Wagtail.

"   "   with Ronald, bright & clear, fish splashing at fly. Only fished 2 hours

Coarse fishing with R.J.F. for 2 hours. (Hemp & bread crust) nothing doing. Saw 16 golden plover.

Spinning for pike for 1½ hrs. River very weedy.

Had 7 rises as well. R.J.F. lost one.

Bitter E. wind, River full of falling leaves & sticks. R.J. only fished short time. Saw 2 green sandpipers.

"   "   "   . Practised spinning. Still too thick with weeds.

"   "   "   "   . Saw a water rail & a lesser spotted Woodpecker & 2 kingfishers.

DATE	WHERE CAUGHT	WATER	RODS	FLY	SALMON	GRILSE	TROUT	SEA TROUT	VARIOUS	WEIGHT LBS.	OZS.
1930	Brought forward.						81	1	9	65	
Nov 7.	Kennet & Canal	N.A.A. water Below Bull's lock.	1						—		
Nov 10	R. Lambourn.	N.A.A. water	1	orange tag			1 put back		—		8
Nov. 11	River Kennet	(Three Fields	1	Blue Phantom					—		
Nov. 12	" "	(Mr Blundell's water)	1						—		
Nov. 13.	Kennet & Canal	N.A.A. Water Below Bull's Lock	1						—		
Nov. 14	River Kennet	Three Fields (Mr Blundell's)	1						—		
Nov. 15	River Kennet	Near Newbury Wharf. White House Bridge	1	Alcock's "True Form" Minnow.					2 perch	2	
Nov. 17	River Kennet.	Mr Trull's Water near Thatcham.		Netting by the Reading Angling Association							

REMARKS

Practising spinning, weeds not down enough.

Rose a good many grayling.

Spinning for pike, Rose a jack.

"   "   ", water much too bright & clear.

"   "   ". Saw 6 golden Plover fly over.

"   "   ". Water very bright & clear, nothing doing.

Grey day. Wind W.

trout, 2 jack, grayling, Roach, dace, perch up to 1½-2 lbs.

	No	Weight	Heaviest fish
Total for 1930			
Sea Trout	1		
Brown "	82	57½	3½.3½.2¾.2½
Pike	1	5½	5½ lbs.
Perch	7	3½	1 lb. 1 oz.
Grayling	3	1	
	94	67½ lbs	

DATE	WHERE CAUGHT	WATER	RODS	FLY	SALMON	GRILSE	TROUT	SEA TROUT	VARIOUS	WEIGHT LBS.	OZS.
1931.		Newbury Angling Ass.							(Thrown back)		
June 2.	River Kennet	below Bull's lock	1	May fly			—		1 Chub		
June 12	Kennet & Avon Canal	Hungerford Canal A.A. Behind Church	1	Red Quill			—		(Thrown back) 1 Grayling		8?
		Total for 1931	2								
1932.											
June. 23	Kennet & Avon Canal	Hungerford Canal AA.	1						—		
" 27	River Kennet	Newbury A.A.	1						—		
Sept 22.	Kennet & Avon Canal	Hungerford Canal A.A.	1						—		
		Total for 1932	0 !!								

Ivy Cottage
Aldbourne
Wilts

REMARKS

Rose a good many, including a very heavy trout. They continually missed the real as well as the artificial fly.

Rose a good many grayling. Saw a quantity of chub, some perch, roach and several jack.

Very hot & thundery. Saw a quantity of chub, perch & jack. A few chub followed the fly. No rise.

Rose a dace, a small trout, then caught, drenched though in a thunderstorm.

Poured with rain all the time. Did not fish very long. Saw a lot of Golden Plover.

DATE 1933.	WHERE CAUGHT	WATER	RODS	FLY	SALMON	GRILSE	TROUT	SEA TROUT	VARIOUS	WEIGHT LBS.	OZS.
May 26.	River Kennet.	Ham Mill	2	May fly.			—		thrown back. 1 dace		
27	" Lambourn	N.A.A. Water.	2				2				
July 12	" Kennet	Ham Mill	2				—				

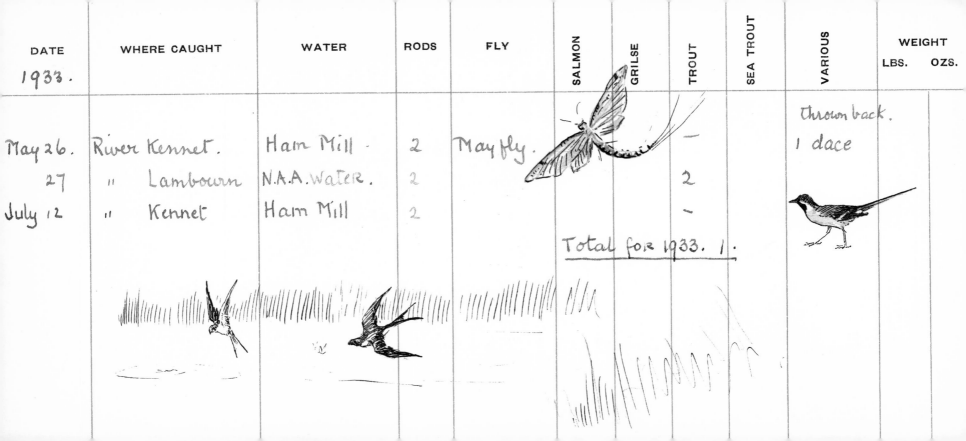

Total for 1933. 1.

REMARKS

air Rise of fly in morning, very few. none in evening, nothing doing. Spinners about. Rose 3 fish in morning, touching 1. R.J.F. 1 dace.
R.J.F one of 11½", self one just under limit. Poured with Rain all the time.
.J.F. & self, nothing doing. Saw grey wagtail - they nested here - also Sandpiper

Ham Mill.

DATE	WHERE CAUGHT	WATER	RODS	FLY	SALMON	GRILSE	TROUT	SEA TROUT	VARIOUS	WEIGHT LBS.	OZS.
1934											
April 9	R. Kennet & Lambourn	Newbury Ang. Ass.	2	Dark Olive			1				
June 9	R. Granta / Old Mill House	The Pool. Below Bridge	1	The Pool. Below Bri:			2		about	—	12
" 10	" " { Hildersham.	Greenhouse Pool.	1				1		"		4
" 11	" " "	Below Bridge	1	Olive			1		"		4
" 13	" " ,	Greenhouse Pool	1				—				
" 14	" " "	The Pool. above Greenhouse Weir	1	Buzz body, dark grey hackle			2		"		8
" 15	" " "	The Pool	1	Small Alder			1			1	10
" 19	" " "	Mill Dam.	1	(Dark) small Sedge (tied by O.B.F)			4			3	3
" 25	" " "	Bridge Pool.	1	'Bloody Butcher'			1				4
							13 (12 by self)			6	13

REMARKS

R.J.F (1), Self touched a small one. No one getting anything. 1st Swallow & Chiffchaff. Grey Wagtail, Ham Mill

Rose a good fish 7 times above the gates. Saw a pair of grey Wagtails - nesting by the Gates

Hooked & lost a good fish in same pool.

Lightly hooked & lost the same fish as on 10th. Close & thundery

After heavy shower. Still very close & thundery succeeding days extremely hot

Fly on the water, Sedge.

Wind W. strong. Largest 1 lb.

Between showers.

DATE	WHERE CAUGHT	WATER	RODS	FLY	SALMON	GRILSE	TROUT	SEA TROUT	VARIOUS	WEIGHT LBS.	OZS.
1934	(Old Mill House				Brought foward		12			6	13
June 26	R. Granta {Hildersham.	Greenhouse Pool .	1	Bloody Butcher .			1				10
„ 27	„ „ Above Linton	Pembroke Fishing Club.	1	Hackle fly .			1	Rainbow Trout			4
„ 30	„ „ Old Mill House	Greenhouse Pool	1				1				8
July 2	„ „ „ „ „	Stream below the Pool	1	Nymph .			—				
July 4	„ „ „ „ „ „	„ „ „ „ „	1	Bloody Butcher.			1				14
July 6.	„ „ „ „ „	Greenhouse Pool.	1						1 Pike.		
Aug 8 - 9	„ „ „ „ „		1				¬				
									.		
		Total for 1934 .					16	Trout, weight		9 lbs	1 o

The long drought & the great amount of flannel weeds, makes fishing very difficult.

ost another Rainbow, saw 2 others, Rainbows, but water far too clear

oo much scum to fish much, very hot.

hooked & lost a fish of about $\frac{3}{4}$ lb.

At 5 A.M. Mist rising like smoke from the River

old Mill House

about 1' long, netted out of pool. It had probably run up from the Lake which is drying up.

River falling fast, water very dead. Occasional slack Rise.

After I left, the River above the gates, dried right up & all the trout there, including many large ones, died. The lake also dried up, but the fish were netted out & taken away in Lorries.

DATE	WHERE CAUGHT	WATER	RODS	FLY	SALMON	GRILSE	TROUT	SEA TROUT	VARIOUS	WEIGHT LBS.	OZS.
1935											
June 7.	R. Lambourn.	N.A.A.	2	May fly.			—				
" 20	R. Granta (Old Mill House	The Pool	1				1				
" 26	" Hildersham)	"	1	Olive			2			1	
July 2	" "	Greenhouse Pool	1	Olive .			1				
" 3	" "	" "	1				1				
" 4	" "	The Pool	1				1				
" 6	" "	Greenhouse Pool	1	Red quill			1				
" 16	" "	" "	1	" "			1			1	12
" 18	" "	Bridge "	1	Olive			1/9		about	5	0

REMARKS

R.J.F 1 small trout. I rose 7 to May fly, splashy rises, not taking the fly at all. No rise of Mayfly.

bout 9", put back. Rain most of the day. heavy & overcast.

argest 10oz. put back the other (about 9")

bout 9"-10", put back. Rose by far the largest trout I ever saw in that pool. Osbern shot a 12" jack in same pool.

Small.

bout 9"-10"

ust under the 11" limit - put back.

fishing very poor owing to extreme

heat.

Old Mill House

WHERE CAUGHT · WATER · RODS · FLY · SALMON · GRILSE · TROUT · SEA TROUT · VARIOUS · WEIGHT · LBS · OZS

The River
at Hildersham

DATE 1936	WHERE CAUGHT	WATER	RODS	FLY	SALMON	GRILSE	TROUT	SEA TROUT	VARIOUS	WEIGHT LBS.	OZS.
June 17.	R. Granta. (Old Mill House) Hildersham.	The Pool	1	Red Quill.			1				5
" 19		" "	1	Wyckham's Fancy			1				12
June 22	"	" "	1	Red Tag			1				12
" 26	"	" "	1				1 Rainbow			1	4
July 7	"	" "	2				1				12
" 11	R. Granta, Linton	(Barcham Hall)	2				2			1	
							7			4	1

Self 4 weighing 3 lbs.

Threw back.

6"

B.F.

B.F. (self none)

Old Mill House
Hildersham.

DATE 1937	WHERE CAUGHT	WATER	RODS	FLY	SALMON	GRILSE	TROUT	SEA TROUT	VARIOUS	WEIGHT LBS.	OZS.
may 14.	River Lambourn	Newbury Angling Ass.	2	Light olive			—				
" 17	" "	" " "	2	" "			1				
" 22	" "	" " "	2	" "			—				
" 25	" "	" " "	2	" "			1				
" 28	" "	" " "	2	" "			1				5
" 31	" "	" " "	2	Dups indispensible			2				
June 15	R. Granta (Old Mill	The Pool	1	Grey Gnat			1				3
16	House, Hildersham)	" "	1	Red Tag			1				14
							6	(self 3)		1	6

REMARKS

O.B.F. & self. Rose 3, cold N.E. wind, only 1 or 2 odd May Flies.

O.B.F. (1) Self (0). Rose 3, hooked & lost one. Wind N.E.O. used a Red fly.

O.B.F. & self. very wet & cold. Wind S.W. nothing doing.

O.B.F. (1) & self. Bright Sun, Rose five. Wind S.W.

O.B.F. (0) & Self (1) Rose 2 others. Hot sun, River very bright & clear.

O.B.F. (2) & Self (0) only Rose 1 fish.. Still no proper Rise of May fly.

DATE 1937	WHERE CAUGHT	WATER	RODS	FLY	SALMON	GRILSE	TROUT	SEA TROUT	VARIOUS	WEIGHT LBS.	OZS.
June 18	R. Granta (Old Mill House Hildusham)	Below the Pool	1	Hares ear			—				
" 19		The Pool & Lower Pools	1	Wickhams Fancy			3			1	10
" 20	"	The Pool	1	"			1				10
" 21	"	Bridge Pool.	1	"			1				4
" 22	"	" " (3) Lower P. "	1	"			5			2	0
" 23	"	Lurn Pool	1	"			1				2?
" 24	"	The Pool	1	"			1				13
" 27	"	Above Bend	1	"			1				3
							13			5	10

Hooked & lost a good one.
Largest 1¼ lb. in the Pool

DATE	WHERE CAUGHT	WATER	RODS	FLY	SALMON	GRILSE	TROUT	SEA TROUT	VARIOUS	WEIGHT LBS.	OZS.
1937											
June 29	R. Granta (Old Mill	The Pool.	1	Wickham's Fancy			—				
" 30	House. Hildasham)	" "	1	"			1				8
July 2	" "	Pool, & Green house P.	1	"			—				6
" 3	"	Lawn Pool.	1	"			1				6
" 4	"	Pool & Bridge Pool.	2	"			2		(1 Rainbow)		6
" 5	"		2				7			1	0
" 8	"	Pool (2) Granary Pet	2				4			3	5
" 11	"	Orchard Ponds	2	Red Gnat			6			1	0
							21	(self 9)		6	9

Hooked, lost a small one.

Hooked & lost 1, Rose 2 others.

Very hot & heavy.

Self Rainbow of $\frac{1}{4}$ lb. R.T.F. small.

R.J.F. all small.

O.B.F 1 lb. in Pool, $1\frac{1}{2}$ lb. Granary Pool, self gog Pool, $\frac{1}{4}$ lb. Greenhouse Pool.

O.B.F. (2) self (4) young trout 6"–7", put into stream that Runs into Pool.

DATE	WHERE CAUGHT	WATER	RODS	FLY	SALMON	GRILSE	TROUT	SEA TROUT	VARIOUS	WEIGHT	
										LBS.	OZS.
1937.											
July 12	R. Granta (old Mill	The Pool.		Red Grat.			1			1	1
" 13	House, Hildersham)	Orchard Ponds.	2	" "			3				8
" 14	Pembroke Fishing Club.	Above Linton	1				1				3 ?
" 15	Hildersham.	The Pool.	1				1	Rainbow			12
Sept 6	"		1				1				4
							7			2	12
							3	— Club Members		2	14
							10			5	10

Mr Henn caught 1 of ¾ lb.   Mine of 1lb.1oz was very game.

O.B. ∋ (1) Self (2) young trout, put into stream which runs into Pool.   Mr Walford (2) in & below Pool. 1lb2oz: 1lb.

Very hot, water very clear, saw some good fish.   Mr Vernon Jones & Son on Hildersham water (0

Before breakfast. All the month, heavy thundery weather. fish in deep water, showing very lit

Total for 1937.	No. 4	Self.	Weight.	Self.
R. Lambourn	4	1	1 lb 4oz	4oz.
R. Granta	46	30	18 14oz.	11·10
	50	31	19 lbs. 14 oz	11 lbs. 14 oz

DATE	WHERE CAUGHT	WATER	RODS	FLY	SALMON	GRILSE	TROUT	SEA TROUT	VARIOUS	WEIGHT LBS.	WEIGHT OZS
1938											
Ap 13–20	R. Granta	Hildersham					—				
June 4	" , Old Mill House -	" Greenhouse Pool	1				1				8
" 5	" "	The Pool & Lower Pools	1	Tinsel Body			3			1	8
" 6	" "	The Pool		"			1				12
" 8	" "	" "	1	Nymph			1	Rainbow		1	12
" 9	" "	" "	1				1				12
" 12	" "	Pond.	1	Nymph			1				4
" 15	" "	"	1				1				4
							9			5	12

Bitterly cold N.E. wind, a blank week.

Hooked & lost a very good fish 1½-2 th. & another of about 3 ... $\frac{3^{lb}}{4}$ Largest 13 oz.

DATE	WHERE CAUGHT	WATER	RODS	FLY	SALMON	GRILSE	TROUT	SEA TROUT	VARIOUS	WEIGHT LBS.	OZ
1938							Brought forward 4			5	12
June 18	R. Granta. Hildersham Pond		1				1				4
" 19	" " "						1				4
" 20	" " "		4				1				4
" 24	" "	Pool & Lower Pool (Bridge)	2				2			1	
" 25	" "	Bridge Pool	3				1 small.				
" 26	" "	Granary Pool							1 pike	3	4
							15 (self 13)		1 pike.	10	12

...ut in Mill Dam.

"

..Perritt, MR Marsh, O. B. F. Self (1) put in Mill Dam.

..T. F (1) Self (1) both ½ lb.

.. Walford (1) R.T.F. & Self only fished a very short time. Fish not Rising well owing to the drought.

.. Rapped by O. B. F. in a pike trap.

DATE 1939	WHERE CAUGHT	WATER	RODS	FLY	SALMON	GRILSE	TROUT	SEA TROUT	VARIOUS	WEIGHT LBS.	OZS
May 3	R. Coln. Fairford. Glos.	"The Bull" water	2				3			1	
June 13	R. Granta. Hildersham	The Pool.	1				—				
" 14	" "	Orchard Ponds	2				2				4
" 15	" "	Mill Dam	2	Hackled Butcher			8		(1 Rainbow)	4	
" "	" "	Orchard Pond									
" 16.	" "	Mill Dam &	1	Hackled Butcher.			4		(1 Rainbow)	1	12
" "	" "	Orchard Pond									
" 17	" "	Lawn &	1	Bloody Butcher			2				12
	" "	Granary Pool					19			7	18

major GREY (2) Self (1) Wind N.E. Bright sun. Fish Rising very short. A very lovely stretch of River.

Hooked & lost a good fish.

Self 1 y 6.B.J. 1. Both small. Mine had no tail at all.

Self 5 in Mill Dam, largest 1½ lbs. & lost a nice Rainbow, all on hackled Butcher. O B J. 3 small i

Orchard Pond. High Wind S.W.

Rainbow 1lb. & Brown Trout from Mill Dam, 2 small from Pond. High Wind S.W.

Wind S.W.

DATE 1939	WHERE CAUGHT	WATER	RODS	FLY	SALMON	GRILSE	TROUT	SEA TROUT	VARIOUS	WEIGHT LBS.	OZS
June 19	R. Granta. Hildersham	Bridge Pool (3)	1	Bloody Butcher			5			2	12
" "	" "	Granary Pool (2)									
" 20	" "	The Pool	1	Bloody Butcher			1 (Rainbow)				4
" 21	" "	Mill Dam	1	Fly Spoon.			1 (Rainbow)				8
" 22	" "	Granary Pool (1)	2	Maid Brown			5			3	
" "	" "	Bridge Pool (2)									
" "	" "	Lawn Pool (2)									
							12			6	8

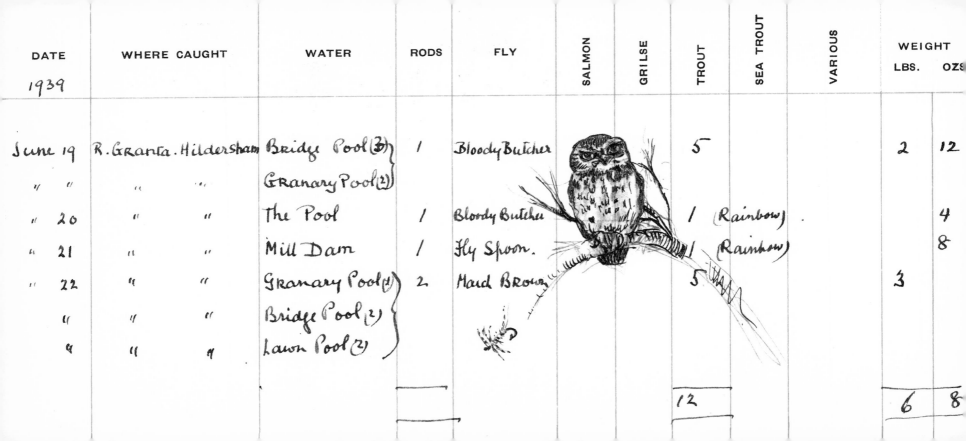

...argest fish 1lb 2 oz. 1lb ,   Wind N W .

Wind N . W .

N.E.   Trying for big ones which O.B.J. wants out of MillDam, but did not Rise any of them.

O.B.F. 19 1lb. Granary Pool, Self 4, 19 1½ lbs in Bridge Pool . Wind N.E .

DATE	WHERE CAUGHT	WATER	RODS	FLY	SALMON	GRILSE	TROUT	SEA TROUT	VARIOUS	WEIGHT LBS.	OZS.
1939.											
June 23	R. Granta. Hildersham	The Pool (2)	2	Grey Gnat.			5		(1 Rainbow.)	4	8
" "	" "	Turn below Pool (2)									
" "	" "	Mill Dam (1)									
" 24	" "	Orchard Pools	2	Grey Gnat			2			~~2~~	8
" "	" "	Granary Pool									
" 25	" "	The Pool r	1	Grey Gnat.			2		(1 Rainbow)	1	
" "	" "	Turn below Pool									
							9			6	

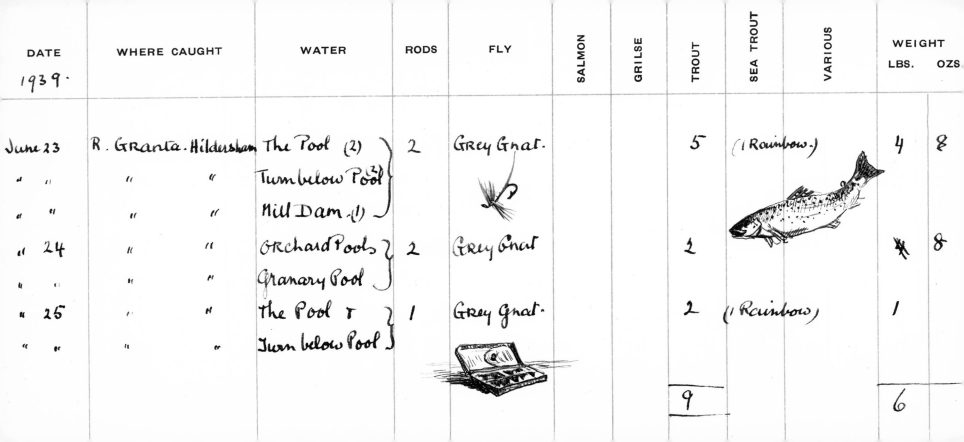

Self 3. 1¼lb. 1lb. & ¾lb. O.B.F. 1 of 1lb in Pool & ½lb Rainbow in Mill Dam. All mine were in Pool or turn below it. Wind N.

O.B.F. & Self. 1 each. Wind N.E.

Rainbow in the Pool. Brown Trout ¾ lb. below Pool. Wind N.N.W. fish came up during a slight shower.

DATE 1939	WHERE CAUGHT	WATER	RODS	FLY	SALMON	GRILSE	TROUT	SEA TROUT	VARIOUS	WEIGHT LBS.	OZS.
June 26.	R. Granta. Hildersham	Turn below Pool	1	Grey Gnat (2)			5	(2 Rainbows)		2	4
" "	" "	Lawn Pool		Hackled fly							
" "	" "	Mill Dam (2)		with white tail }							
" 27.	" "	" "	2				3	(1 Rainbow)			14
" "	" "	Granary Pool.									
" 29	" "	Turn below Pool	1	Greenwell's glory			2			1	
July 2	" "	Greenhouse Pool	1				1				2?
							11			4	4

Largest Rainbow 1¼ lbs. both Rainbows where on white tailed fly ♀ from Mill Dam.
Wind N. W.   Saw a Water Shrew behind Granary

Water Shrew.

½ lb. Brown & 4 lb Rainbow by Self in Mill Dam.   O. B. J. (Small) Granary Pool.
I have never known the Mill Dam fish so well, the incessant high wind kept down the
Wind W. S. W.   L flannel weed & kept a good Ripple.

DATE	WHERE CAUGHT	WATER	RODS	FLY	SALMON	GRILSE	TROUT	SEA TROUT	VARIOUS	WEIGHT LBS. OZS.
1939 June 13 – July 2	R. Granta, Hildersham. Cambs.	O.B.F.'s water.		48 trout weighing 23½ lbs. O.B.F. who did not fish The largest trout were 1½ lb. 1½ lb. 1¼ lb. 1¼ lb. 1 lb 2 ozs;						

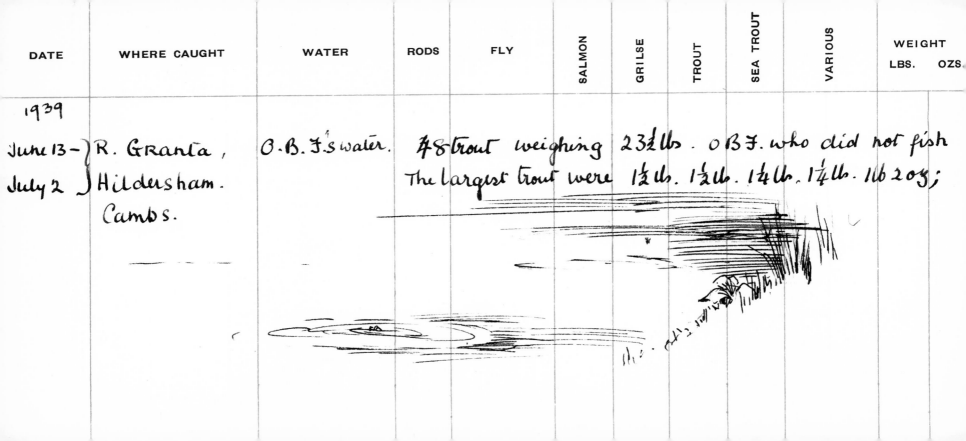

much, caught 9 & self 39 (which weighed 20¾ lbs) Of these, 9 were Rainbows, self 8, O.B.I.

1 lb. 1 lb. 1 lb. (by Self.) & 1 lb. 1 lb. (by O.B.I.)

Analysis of Pools.

Mill Dam.	13 fish	Bridge Pool.	5
The Pool	5	Lawn Pool.	4
Turn below Pool.	6	Green house Pool	1
Granary Pool.	6	Orchard Ponds.	7

DATE 1946	WHERE CAUGHT	WATER	RODS	FLY	SALMON	GRILSE	TROUT	SEA TROUT	VARIOUS	WEIGHT LBS. OZS.
May 14.	Hildersham, River Granta	The Pool	1	Red Quill			4			
May 17	" "	" "	1	Red Quill			—			
May 18	" "	" "	1	march Brown			2			
May 19	" "	" "	2	march Brown			2			
May 20	" "	" "	1	Grey Hackle			2			
							10 (9 by self)			about 3 LBS.

REMARKS

The first time I have fished since the War.

N.—N.W. cold

hooked & lost a fish.

S.E.

O.B.F. 1 of 1 LB. Self 1, hooked & lost 4 more. Rain most of day. N.E. Thunder.

S.

DATE 1947	WHERE CAUGHT	WATER	RODS	FLY	SALMON	GRILSE	TROUT	SEA TROUT	VARIOUS	WEIGHT LBS.	OZS
	Hildersham. Cambs.										
May 14	~~River~~ Granta	The Pool	1	Grey Quill			1				12
" 15	River Granta	The Pool (4)	2	Grey Quill &			6			4	4
		Greenhouse Pool (1)		Orange Tag							
		Granary Pool (1)									
May 16.	River Granta	The Pool	1	Blue Upright			4			2	4
		Granary Pool		(hackle)							
		Greenhouse "		"							
								.			
							11 (1 by O.B.F.)			7 LBS.	4

B.F. fished for a short time, 1 of 4 LB. in Granary Pool. Self. ¾ LB ½ LB 7 2 of ½ LB in the Pool & 1 of ½ LB by green houses. O.B.F. is not fishing much, since the accident to his leg.

LB in the Pool. ¾ LB, ½ LB in Granary Pool. 4 LB Greenhouse Pool.

DATE	WHERE CAUGHT	WATER	RODS	FLY	SALMON	GRILSE	TROUT	SEA TROUT	VARIOUS	WEIGHT	
										LBS.	OZS
1947					Brought forward.		11			7	4
May 17	River Granta	The Pool	1	Blue Upright			3			2	3
" "	" "	Granary Pool		(hackle)							
" "	" "	Greenhouse "		"							
May 18	River Granta	The Pool	1	Blue Upright			1				4
" 19	" "	The Pool	1	Small Partridge			3			1	4
" "	" "	Bridge Pool		& Orange.							
" "	" "	Greenhouse Pool									
							18 trout			10 LBS	15 oz

of 1LB 9oz between Granary Pool & the Pool, worked him up into the Pool & landed him there.

½ LB. Granary Pool & a small fish in the Greenhouse Pool.

LB. ½ LB. ¼ LB.   The River is in very good order after the severe winter floods, there is a good stock of fish, in good condition, & more fish showing between the Mill dam & the Fish Walk. The last days of my week were very cold & very little fly about. Saw a Sandpiper

self #617 trout weighing 10¾ LBS

DATE 1948	WHERE CAUGHT	WATER	RODS	FLY	SALMON	GRILSE	TROUT	SEA TROUT	VARIOUS	WEIGHT LBS.	OZS
	Hildersham. Cambs.	3 in the Pool		3 on Olive							
May 11	R. Granta	1 in Granary Pool	1	1 on a blackfly			4			1	12
" 12	" "	The Pool	1				1				9
" 13	" "						—				
" 14	" "		1	Ginger hackle "Osbern's Fly"			1				12
" 15	" "	Granary Pool	1				2			1	
" 16	" "	The Pool	1	"Osbern's Fly"			2			1	4
							10			5	5

REMARKS

2 put back.) Caught them all as a thunderstorm was coming up.
Cold evening, no proper Rise.
Saw 5 Mayfly, they had not been seen here for many years.
his dressing was taught O.B.F. by Patterson, the old man (now dead) who made Rods
or Ogden Smith's. It is a very sparse dressing ⟶⟋⟋⟋⟋⟋⟋⟋⟋   ⟋⟋⟋⟋⟋⟋ the tip of the
hackle feather for the tail & the hackle twisted on top of the silk body.
his fly was a ginger Jungle Cock feather tied with primrose silk. No 2. hook
and NE. very few fish Rising, Brilliant sunshine. a lot of wind. Nothing over $\frac{3}{4}$ LB.

DATE	WHERE CAUGHT	WATER	RODS	FLY	SALMON	GRILSE	TROUT	SEA TROUT	VARIOUS	WEIGHT LBS	OZS
1949											
May 10	Granary Pool.	R. Granta. Camb	1				1			1	
May 11.	The Pool.	" "	1				1			1	
June 1.	Dead Man's Pool,	Llanberis.	1				—				
" "	Llyn Padarn,	Caernarvon, N. Wales	2				—				

ust under 14B. (Borrowed Rod etc from O.B.F. as just had most of my tackle stolen)

ver 1LB. a long, narrow fish.

very deep, black little lake, surrounded by trees or cliff. difficult to fish.

ery deep - 3½ miles long - a most beautiful lake. (With Squadron Leader & Ilga Stoltz, Mr Curry)

FINIS
ARTHRITIS!

DUNDONNELL
IN MARCH.

Year	Salmon	Heaviest Salmon	Sea Trout	Heaviest Sea Trout	Brown Trout	Heaviest Trout	Rainbow Trout	Heaviest Rainbow	Grayling	Char	Saithe (Coal fish)	Cod	Lythe	Haddock	Flounder	Whiting	Sea Bream	Red Gurnet	Grey Gurnet	Mackerel	Sundries	Weight lbs	oz	Total for year	Remarks
1913					8						5	11		10	1	18	1	1	2		1 Dab.	20?		58	
1915					93	1¾lbs					4	2		2	1							52 (about)		102	Largest coal fish 10lbs.
1916	2		9	1½	100	1½lbs					9	1		1		1			1			103	8	124	
1917	4	18lbs	35	3lbs	147	4¼lbs					19											229	4	205	2 largest trout 4¼ lbs each, Sea Trout 3 lbs, Coal fish 7 lbs
1918	1	4lbs	14	2½lb	22	1½lbs																53	4	37	
1919	3	9½lbs	27	2½lb	107	1¾lbs					12											169		149 (219 self)	Coal fish 8 lbs.
1920	1	11½lbs	2		23						4	68	1	42	11	382 (not all by self)			8		36 (Cuddie)	232	4	619	Not all by self. Cod of 7lbs
1921			2		49	1½lbs						12	2	6		3				12		25 (about)		103	9 Coal fish 8 Lbs (self.)
1922					22										5						82	24?		109	Not all by self, plaice Wrasse, Pouting etc
1923			22	1¾	42	1¼lbs														45	2	64		111	
1924					61	¾lb				2												19	8	63	
Totals	11		111		674					2	53	94	3	61	18	404	1	1	11	57	121	991	12	1680	

Year	Salmon	Heaviest	Sea Trout	Heaviest	Brown Trout	Heaviest	Rainbow Trout	Heaviest	Char	Grayling	Pike	Heaviest	Perch	Chub				Bass	Cod	Coal Fish (Saithe)	Lythe	Haddock	Flounder	Whiting	Sea Bream	Red Gurnet	Grey Gurnet	Mackerel
Brought Forward	11	18lbs	111	3lb	674	4½lbs			2										94	53	3	61	18	404	1	1	11	57
1925					97	3 lbs.																	3					
1926			8	5lbs10oz	111	1lb.13oz	33	10oz												41	1							
1927					159	1lb.	12	8oz										1										
1928					104	1¼lb.	2	14oz		1																		
1929	1	21 lbs			68	3¾lb	2	6oz.			4	16lbs																
1930			1		82	3½lb	—			3	1	5½lbs	7															
1931										1				1														
1932																												
1933					1																							
	12	21lb	120	5lb10	1296	4½lbs	49	14oz	2	5	5	16lbs	7	1				1	94	94	4	61	21	404	1	1	11	57

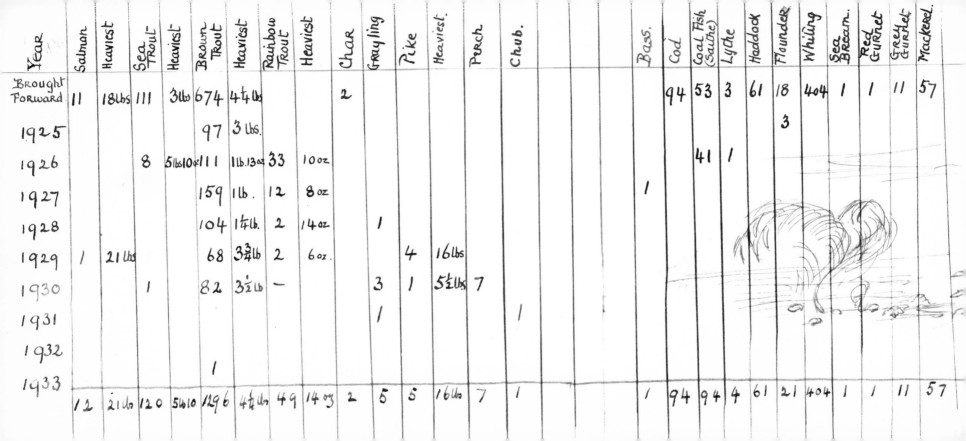

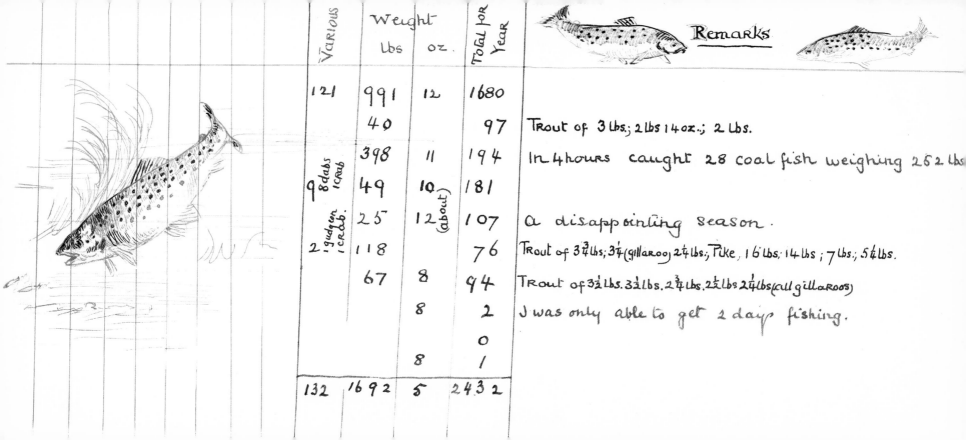

Various	Weight lbs	Weight oz.	Total for Year	 Remarks 
121	991	12	1680	
	40		97	Trout of 3 lbs.; 2 lbs 14 oz.; 2 lbs.
	398	11	194	In 4 hours caught 28 coal fish weighing 262 lbs
9 (8 dabs 1 crab)	49	10	181	
	25	12 (about)	107	A disappointing season.
2 (1 gudgeon 1 crab.)	118		76	Trout of $3\frac{3}{4}$ lbs; $3\frac{1}{4}$ (gillaroo) $2\frac{1}{4}$ lbs.; Pike, 16 lbs; 14 lbs; 7 lbs.; $5\frac{1}{4}$ lbs.
	67	8	94	Trout of $3\frac{1}{2}$ lbs. $3\frac{1}{2}$ lbs. $2\frac{3}{4}$ lbs. $2\frac{1}{2}$ lbs $2\frac{1}{4}$ lbs (all gillaroos)
		8	2	I was only able to get 2 days fishing.
			0	
		8	1	
132	1692	5	2432	

Year	Salmon	Heaviest Salmon	Sea Trout	Heaviest Sea Trout	Rainbow Trout	Brown Trout	Char	Grayling	Pike	Heaviest Pike	Heaviest Brown Trout	Perch	Chub	Cod	Coal Fish (Scuthe)	Pollack (Lythe)	Bass
Brought forward	12	21 lbs	120	5lb10	49	1296	2	5	5	16 lbs	4¼lb.	7	1	94	94	4	1
1934					1	15					1lb10.						
1935						9					1 lb.						
1936.					1	3					1¼ (rainbow)						
1937					2	29					1¼						
1938					1	12					1¾ (rainbow)						
1939					8	32					1½						
1940 – 1945. no fishing owing to the war																	
1946						9											
1947						17					1lb9oz						

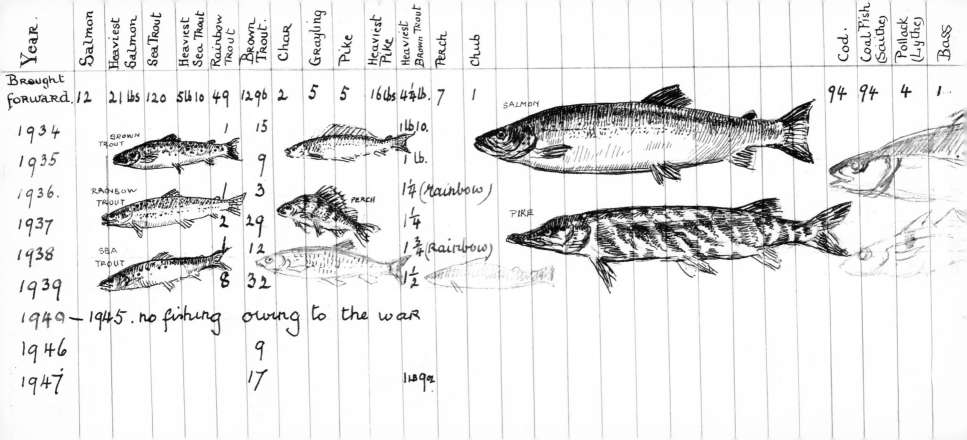

Haddock	Plaice	Flounder	Whiting	Sea Bream	Gurnard	Mackerel	Various	Weight lbs.	oz	Total	Remarks
61		21	404	1	12	57	132	1692	5	2432	
								9	1	16	Fishing very bad. second year of drought.
								5		9	" " " , not Recovered from drought
								3		4	" " " , much better late in season, after I left.
								11	14	31	1¼ lbs: 1lb. 1oz: 14 oz: 13 oz: 13 oz: 12 oz (Rainbow)
								7		13	1¾ lbs. Rainbow
								21		40	1½; 1½; 1¼; 1¼ Rainbow; 1lb. 2 oz; 1; 1; 1;
								3		9	
								10	4	17	1 lb 9 oz.: ¾ lb. ¾ lb. ¾ lb. ¾ lb. Much better than last year

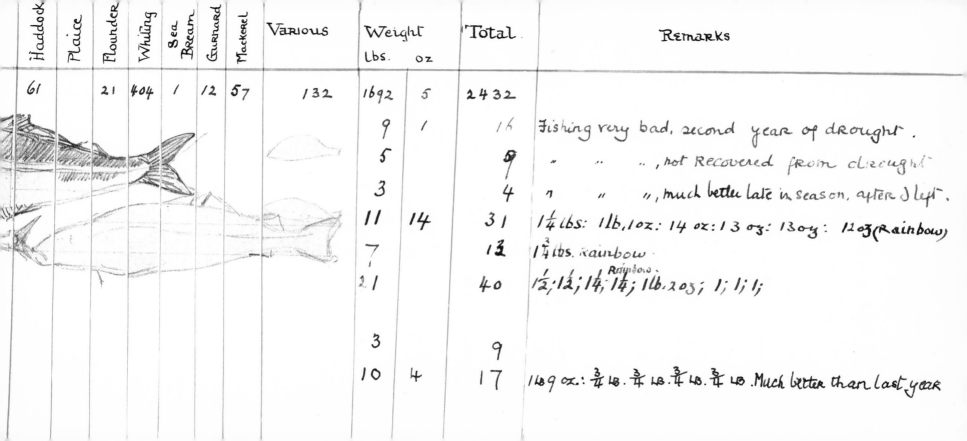

Brown Trout of 1 lb & upwards. (underlined in red caught by self)

Loch a Charn. Dundonnell. Ross. 1¼; 2 lbs. 1 oz.; 1¾; 1¼; 2; 1 lb 13 oz; 1; 1; 1¼; 1¾ (1915); 1½; 1 lb 7; 1 lb 2; 1 lb 2; 1; 1½; 32 weighing 28 lbs. 4 of 1½ (1922) 1¼; 1¼; 1; (192

Loch an Fraoich, " " . 1; 1½; 1; 1; 1½; 1 (1919) 1½; 1½; 2; 1¼; 1 lb 10 oz. (1925)

Loch an Buidhe " " 1½ (1915); 1 (1919).

Loch nam Badan Bog-a. " 1½: (1916) 7 fish 9 lbs (1½, 1½, 1 lb 3; 1 lb 1 oz), 3 fish 1¼, 1¼, 1¼; 1 lb; 1¼; (1917) 1 lb 6; 2 fish 2¾; 10 fish 11½, 8 fish 9¼; 2 lbs 6; (1925) 1¾; 1½,

Waterlily Loch " (1917) 4 fish 1½, 1¼, 1¼, 1¼; 2 fish 1¼, 1¼; 1¼; (1918) 1½; (1925) 3¼; 3½;

Loch on Meall an drean " (1917) 4 lbs 4 oz; 4 lbs. 4 oz. The only fish ever caught here

Reedy Loch. (L. Dhu) " 1½; 1; 1¾; 1¾; 1 lb. 2 oz; 2 fish, 1¾, 1 lb (1919)

Artificial Loch (Loch Broom Glebe) 4 fish between 3-4 lbs each. Since then cleaned out by poachers

L. an Tiompain " " " 3 fish of 2¾ each (with L. a Mhill); 8 fish. 14 lbs (1919); 1½ (1921) 1 lb (1925)

L. an Fhion " " " 4 lbs 1 oz.; 1½; 1 lb.

L. a Mhill " " " (1921) 3 lbs 2 oz; 4 of 1½ each; (1925) 2 lbs, 14 oz.; 3 lbs.

Little Loch a Charn " " " 6 lbs

Loch Farraline. Strath Errick. Inverness (1925) 2 lbs.

Loch Garth   "   "   (1925) 1 lb. 3 oz.

Loch an Urigh, (Mystery L.) "   "   (1927) 1 lb.

Dundonnell River. Ross.   (1917) 1 lb 10 oz; (1925) 3¼ lb.

R. Granta. Cambs.   1 lb. 2 oz. (1926) 1 lb 13; 1¼; 1¾; 1¾; 1¾; 1½; 1½; 1;1; 2 lbs (Rainbow) (1929) 1. (1934) 1 lb 10 oz. 1 lb (1936) 1¼ lb

Lough Columbkille. Donegal.   (1928) 1 lb 4 oz.;

Lough Conn. Co. Mayo. (1929) 1 lb; 1¾ lb; 1 lb; 1¾; 3¾; 3¼ (gillaroo) 1½; 1 lb; 1 lb; 1 lb; 4 lbs.; 1 lb; 1¼; 1; 3½ lbs. 1½. 2¼; 4 l

Lough Cullen. Co. Mayo (1929) 1¼; 1¼ (1930) 1¼; 3

Lough Conn (1930) 3; 1¼; 1; 1; 1 lb 6 oz (gillaroo); 1; 3 lb 4 oz; 2½; 1 lb 6 oz (gillaroo); 2½; 2½; 1 lb 10 oz. 1 lb. 2¼ lb (gillaroo) 1; 1¼; 2½ + 3½ lb (gillaroos)

"   "   1 lb 7 oz; 1¼; 1¼; 1; 1; 1¾; 2¾ (gillaroo) 3½ lb (gillaroo)

R. Granta. 1¼ lbs; 1 lb 10 oz. 1 lb; 1 lb; 1½ lbs; (1937) 1¼ lb; 1 lb; 1¼ lb; 1 lb; 1¾ (Rainbow), 1938. 1½; 1½; 1; 1; 1; 1¼ (Rainbow) 1½; 1; 1 lb (Rainbow) 1½ lb; 14 oz; 1¼ lb. 1939 1 lb. 9 oz. 1947: June 1955, 3½ lbs, 11" Round & 21" long.

Weights of Salmon or Trout for inches of length, based on supposition that a salmon of 36" weighs 20 lbs, a Trout of 18", 2½

Measurement from end of snout to middle Ray of tail.

INCHES.		lb.	oz.	INCHES.		LB.	oz.	INCHES.		L.B. oz.	INCHES.		LB. oz.
9	Trout	0	5	21	Trout	4	0	32	Salmon	14.046	44	Salmon	36.516
10	"	0	7	22	"	4	9	33	"	15.404	45	"	39.063
11	"	0	9	23	"	5	3	34	"	16.848	46	"	41.725
12	"	0	12	24	"	5	15	35	"	18.379	47	"	44.506
13	"	0	15	25	"	6	11	36	"	20	48	"	47.407
14	"	1	3	26	"	7	8	37	"	21.713	49	"	50.432
15	"	1	7	27	"	8	7	38	"	23.522	50	"	53.584
16	"	1	12	28	"	9	6	39	"	25.428	51	"	56.864
17	"	2	2	29	"	10	7	40	"	27.435	52	"	60.274
18	"	2	8	30	"	11	9	41	"	29.544	53	"	63.819
19	"	2	15	30	Salmon	11.574	42	"	31.759	54	"	67.500
20	"	3	7	31	"	12.770	43	"	34.082	55	"	71.320

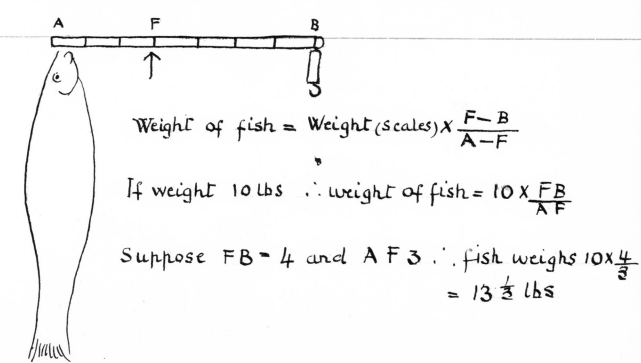

$$\text{Weight of fish} = \text{Weight (scales)} \times \frac{F-B}{A-F}$$

If weight 10 lbs $\therefore$ weight of fish $= 10 \times \dfrac{FB}{AF}$

Suppose $FB = 4$ and $AF\ 3$ $\therefore$ fish weighs $10 \times \dfrac{4}{3}$

$$= 13\tfrac{1}{3} \text{ lbs}$$

Not at once of Test and Itchen
  Sing I, nor of Kennet's state
Whence my fario come to kitchen
  Salmon-pink and grampus-great;
But, though Berkshire's bulrush quivers,
  But, though Hampshire's kingcup's out,
First I'll sing of little rivers
  And of very little trout.

Little trout whose claims do beckon
  So insistently and sound
Little trout whose bulk we reckon
  Six or seven to the pound —
These I'll sing, to these beholden
  These long since a song did earn
Crimson-spotted, plump and golden
  Flung a-kicking from the burn.

Leaping down the brown hill's shoulder
  Trailed of birk and mountain ash;
Bent upon by granite boulder,
  Little waters hop and splash;
Pied by snows of last December,
  Bens above the May days flout —
Ah! that's how you'll best remember
  Little rivers, little trout!

Grease your brogues with dreamland tallow,
  Forth with me and fish like kings,
And by pot and swirling shallow
  Fill a creel with fingerlings,
Where our noses first got blistered,
  Where our greenhearts first went "swish,"
Where the paws of boyhood glistered
  With the scales of little fish.

Those were days, you say? Why then it
  Scarce is odd if thus I wink,
Ere we walk by lovely Kennet,
  Ere we follow Itchen's brink,
Where the Berkshire bulrush quivers,
  Where the Hampshire kingcup's out,
Wink with love at little rivers
  And at very little trout.